The
PRODUCTION
NOTEBOOKS

The
$\mathcal{P}$RODUCTION
NOTEBOOKS

THEATRE IN PROCESS

Volume 1

EDITED, WITH AN INTRODUCTION BY

MARK BLY

"The Clytemnestra Project" at The Guthrie Theater
By Jim Lewis

Danton's Death at Alley Theatre
By Christopher Baker

The Love Space Demands at Crossroads Theatre Company
By Shelby Jiggetts

Children of Paradise: Shooting a Dream at Theatre de la Jeune Lune
By Paul Walsh

THEATRE COMMUNICATIONS GROUP

Copyright © 1996 by Mark J. Bly

The Production Notebooks: Theatre in Process, Volume 1 is published by
Theatre Communications Group, Inc., 355 Lexington Ave., New York, NY 10017-0217.

"The Clytemnestra Project" by Jim Lewis, photographs copyright © 1996
by Michal Daniel; costume sketches copyright © 1996 by Susan Hilferty.

Danton's Death by Christopher Baker, production photographs copyright © 1996
by Jim Caldwell; production photographs copyright © 1996 by T. Charles Erickson. All
design sketches and drawings are copyright © by Robert Wilson, RW Work Ltd, and are
reprinted by permission of Byrd Hoffman Foundation: photograph of *The President's Chair*
copyright © 1996 by Paul Hester.

The Love Space Demands by Shelby Jiggetts, production photographs copyright © 1996
by Rich Pipeling Photography, Oldwick, NJ; projection photographs
copyright © 1996 by Adál.

Children of Paradise: Shooting a Dream by Paul Walsh, photographs copyright © 1996
by Michal Daniel.

The Literary Managers and Dramaturgs of the Americas (LMDA) was instrumental
in the promoting and funding of this project.

    The production notebooks / edited and with an introduction by Mark Bly.
    ISBN 1-55936-110-7
    1. Theater—Production and direction. 2. Dramaturges—United States—Diaries.
    I. Bly, Mark. II. Series.
    PN2053.P75   1996
    792'.0232—dc20   95-45987
    CIP

Cover art is from the Alley Theatre production of *Danton's Death* and is reprinted
courtesy of the photographer, T. Charles Erickson copyright © 1996.

Book and cover design by Lisa Govan

First Edition, November 1996

C O N T E N T S

ACKNOWLEDGMENTS

This book would not have been possible without the commitment, cooperation and generosity of a large number of people. I am extremely grateful to the artistic directors, stage directors, various artists, technicians and theatre staffs who produced, staged and participated in the creation of the work described in this volume. I would especially like to thank Garland Wright, Gregory Boyd, Robert Wilson, Robert Auletta, Ricardo Khan, Talvin Wilks, Ntozake Shange, Sydné Mahone, Dominique Serrand, Barbra Berlovitz Desbois, Vincent Gracieux, Robert Rosen, Steven Epp, Felicity Jones, Michael Lupu, Belinda Westmaas, Michal Daniel, Adál, Rich Pipeling, Jim Caldwell, T. Charles Erickson and the Byrd Hoffman Foundation.

    I owe a great debt of gratitude to Anne Cattaneo, Don Shewey, Vicky Abrash, Tim Sanford and Erin Sanders. Anne, as President of Literary Managers and Dramaturgs of the Americas (LMDA), was instrumental in promoting this project and in helping to locate the funding which gave it life. Don's early and enthusiastic response to my 1990 dramaturg's log for *Leon & Lena (and lenz)* (*Theater*, Winter/Spring 1990), kept alive my dream of similar future notebooks. Vicky, Tim and Erin, as past and current presidents of LMDA, have been the calm voices at the other end of the phone line, patiently listening to my latest problem. Anne Cattaneo and Don Shewey served as advisors on this volume. I was always grateful knowing that I could call upon their expertise when I needed advice or a practiced eye.

I would also like to thank Emily Morse of the LMDA office for her endless patience and assistance in response to my interminable questions; and Merv Antonio for his good humor and unfailing help while he was my literary/dramaturgy intern at the Seattle Repertory Theatre.

Major funding for this book was provided by the Andrew W. Mellon Foundation. Additional funding was provided by the Ettinger Foundation. Without the generosity of these organizations, there would be no first volume of *The Production Notebooks*. I am deeply grateful for the opportunity they provided. I believe that the documentation these grants made possible will serve many future generations of historians, critics, educators, students and audiences. I would like to thank Rachel Newton Bellow of the Mellon Foundation, for her generous help and advice; Rocco Landesman for his prescient backing and promotion of yet another theatrical "dark horse"; and Cynthia Mayeda, formerly of the Dayton Hudson Foundation, for many years of friendship, generosity and acute insights.

I appreciate the expertise, perseverance and support of Lindy Zesch, Terence Nemeth, Steven Samuels and Kathy Sova of Theatre Communications Group. I am particularly grateful that they recognized the potential value of this work. I thank Peggy Marks of New York City (a member of the LMDA board of directors) and my lawyer, Mary R. Norris of New Haven, who served as guides through the legal labyrinths. Their skills, judgment and boundless patience helped us find our way through the maze.

I am very grateful to my close friend Pamela Anderson, who acted as associate editor for this volume and assisted me at every stage of this project, from the initial proposals and contracts, through the editorial process, to the final drive to pull together all the details of an effort involving multiple authors and several institutions.

Finally, I am most appreciative of the four dramaturgs who made this volume possible through their energy, intelligence and artistic acumen: Jim Lewis, Chris Baker, Shelby Jiggetts and Paul Walsh. The best testaments to their professional qualifications are the notebooks that follow.

I dedicate this book to the memory of Od Odson and Steven Edmundson, who were two of the earliest, strongest and most vital influences on my life.

The woof of time is every instant broken and the track of generations effaced. Those who went before are soon forgotten; of those who will come after, no one has any idea: the interest of man is confined to those in close propinquity to himself.

—ALEXIS DE TOCQUEVILLE

When you read your parts
Exploring, ready to be surprised,
Look for the new and the old.
As the people say, at the moon's change of phases,
The new moon for one night
Holds the old in its arms.

—BERTOLT BRECHT

"Looking for the New and the Old"
Translated by Paul Walsh

INTRODUCTION

In the 1980s at the Guthrie Theater, whenever my associate Michael Lupu or I finished our involvement with a production of note, we would sit in our seats on closing night protesting silently the passing away of that unique theatrical experience. Frequently, the work was a staging by one of the Romanian exiles, either Lucian Pintilie, known for his innovative postmodern direction of Molière, Chekhov or Ibsen; or Liviu Ciulei, the Guthrie's gifted and wise artistic director. On other occasions, the production had been staged by a leading American avant-garde director, perhaps JoAnne Akalaitis, a co-founder of the Mabou Mines theatre company; Richard Foreman, a founder of the Ontological-Hysteric Theater; or Peter Sellars, the impish director who became known internationally for his imaginative stagings of Shakespeare, Gershwin and Mozart. Of course, the usual archival materials (one or two grainy videotapes, some promptbooks, a smattering of reviews and photographs) remained after the production closed; but little except a few scattered memories survived to retrace the day-to-day creative process, the invisible artistic achievements forged in rehearsals.

Nor, as I have discovered, is such a dearth of documentation rare in the United States. Over the past few years, our theatre community has created some remarkable, imaginatively conceived work, and yet little exists that chronicles these thought-provoking explorations. At best, only faint traces and shadowy impressions of an artistic journey witnessed by a select few remain behind.

So when Anne Cattaneo, the newly elected president of the

Literary Managers and Dramaturgs of the Americas (LMDA), asked me in 1990 what endeavors the organization should be backing, I didn't hesitate: I envisioned a series of casebooks, dedicated to recording the creative processes of major theatre artists and the evolution of noteworthy productions. The four production notebooks which follow are the first of our efforts.

The primary criterion for inclusion in the project is simple: the individuals collaborating on the production must be artists of consequence who have a history of imaginatively conceived productions. An additional practical requirement is the availability of a writer, versed in all aspects of theatre, with superior analytical and writing skills, who would be intimately involved in the work from conception through closing. Fortunately, most major regional theatres today already employ artists, known as "dramaturgs," who meet these criteria. A final requisite is that both the director and the producing theatre agree to allow descriptions of private meetings and rehearsals to be published.

It does not matter whether the resulting staging receives critical approbation. The work of these artists merits documentation whether the final production is acclaimed a success or a failure. We are interested in the evolution of the project, particularly discussions of the obstacles encountered, temporary aesthetic detours and artistic choices made. I envisioned that the production notebooks would illuminate the process of collaboration, offering rare windows into the creative lives of some of North and South America's finest theatre artists.

I anticipated that a notebook might contain (depending on the availability or the relevance to a particular production) a wide spectrum of information: the pre-rehearsal planning and shaping of the overall vision or approach to the play; the evolution of the staged text, particularly in the development of a new script; the chronicling of the day-to-day rehearsal process; notes on the performance run; observations by the participating artists; notes of a more theoretical or critical nature on the staging; commentary on and examples of graphic, film, literary or musical elements contributed by the production dramaturg to augment and inspire the creative work of the other artists; design sketches; rehearsal and performance photographs; graphic elements from the program and poster; program articles and seminal bibliographical entries. Not every rehearsal would need to be included in the final draft of the notebook nor would journals brimming with intrigue and gossip be encouraged.

Obviously, a residual effect of *The Production Notebooks* will be the promotion of a greater awareness of the creative work being done in the Americas today by dramaturgs. Having worked as a dramaturg in regional theatre for fifteen years, I am eager to share this knowledge with others.

Dramaturgy is a relatively new vocation in America, and even among working artists the exact scope and methodology of the dramaturg's professional duties have been subjects of hot debate. A brief historical sketch of the origins of the profession may help to explain some of its current permutations, quandaries and potential.

The eighteenth-century German playwright/critic Gotthold Ephraim Lessing (1729–1781) is generally regarded as the father of the dramaturgy profession, although the functions of the dramaturg have been performed by others throughout theatrical history. In 1767, the unemployed Lessing was hired by the newly founded Hamburg National Theatre, ostensibly to write plays for the burgeoning enterprise. When Lessing balked at the notion of being a perpetual-motion writing machine, the theatre's financial backers asked Lessing to serve as an in-house critic and to write commentary for a newly created journal. Lessing's employers no doubt assumed that he would function as a glorified publicity director, but his collection of 104 essays, which came to be known as *The Hamburg Dramaturgy*, was hardly laudatory.

Lessing was (as the United States dramaturg Joel Schechter notes) the "first [dramaturg] to be critical of his own theatre and its role in society" (*Theater*, Fall 1978, p. 5). His essays were so candid that offended actresses in the company demanded a moratorium on all acting commentary. After the twenty-fifth essay, Lessing concentrated on discussions of Aristotelian and Neoclassical theory, emphasizing the need for native German playwriting. He championed Shakespeare's works in the face of the then-fashionable adulation of French dramas, particularly those by Voltaire and Corneille. Within two years the Hamburg National Theatre, with its dream of creating a permanent repertory company, was bankrupt due primarily to mismanagement. Lessing resigned, but his impact on the future evolution of dramaturgy is undeniable.

Lessing spawned a rogue's gallery of dramaturgical progeny: Ludwig Tieck and Otto Brahm in the nineteenth century; in post-World War I Germany, Carl Zuckmayer and Bertolt Brecht (who served as a dramaturg at Max Reinhardt's Deutsches Theater, and at the Piscator Stage in the 1920s, where he developed his epic theatre theories); Joachim Tenschert, the first dramaturg at Brecht's Berliner Ensemble in the 1950s; and, more recently, Hermann Beil, Heiner Müller, Botho Strauss, Dieter Sturm, Vera Sturm and Ursula Voss. Despite Lessing's ostensibly inauspicious debut as a dramaturg, over the past two centuries the presence of dramaturgs has been an integral part of the evolution of German theatre. This is especially true for resident repertory theatres dedicated to developing and producing new plays and reinvestigating and rethinking the classics.

In the United States, the very earliest seeds of the future profession of dramaturgy probably were sown when the critic/translator William Archer and the Shakespearean director Harley Granville Barker included in their *Scheme and Estimates for a National Theatre* (1904) a proposal for the creation of the new position of literary manager. This *Scheme*, which was for a British national theatre, was published in the United States in 1908. In 1909 another institution, the New Theatre, was dedicated in New York City with the financial backing of the Astor, Morgan and Vanderbilt families. The organization was headed by Winthrop Ames, who clearly was familiar with Archer and Granville Barker's *Scheme*. Ames hired as his literary manager John Corbin, drama critic for *Harper's Weekly* and the *New York Sun*. Corbin was not only the first literary manager in America, but since Archer and Granville Barker had not yet established their National Theatre in England, Corbin also had the honor of becoming the first known literary manager in the English-speaking world. (Laurence Shyer has thoroughly documented these events in *Theater*, Fall 1978.) Corbin's job profile is still recognizable today:

> The Literary Manager shall examine all plays sent to the Theatre and indicate to the Reading Committee such as seem to him worthy of their consideration. It shall further be his duty, subject to the Director, to follow the course of dramatic art in foreign countries, suggest foreign or old plays for revival, and give such aid in revision, arrangement and translation of plays, and such advice on questions of history, archaeology and English as may be required.

But within two years Corbin had resigned, his eyes red-rimmed and bleary from reading and evaluating nearly two thousand plays without discovering any new writers of stature. Corbin's position was abolished and the New Theatre closed shortly thereafter due to public indifference.

Over the next fifty years, the position of literary manager went into hibernation, resurfacing occasionally in various guises. The legendary "play doctors" George S. Kaufman, Moss Hart and

George Abbott rewrote many third acts and performed recon-
structive surgery on ailing scripts; and in the 1920s and 1930s John
Gassner and Francis Fergusson were astute play readers for the
Theatre Guild and the American Laboratory Theatre.

During the 1960s the position of literary manager was revi-
talized in the United States in response to the needs of the burgeoning not-for-profit resident theatre movement. The resident
theatres were committed to developing new plays and reexamin-
ing the classics. Like the New Theatre a half century before, they
were flooded with scripts. The theatres recognized the need for a
resident specialist with artistic, analytical and play development
skills who could help locate scripts which would fulfill or enhance
the artistic director's vision. The individuals hired to fill these positions were referred to as literary advisors or literary managers, with
a nod to their counterparts in British theatres, including the critic
and influential theatrical advisor Kenneth Tynan, who worked as
literary manager with Sir Laurence Olivier at the National Theatre.

In addition, other influences were appearing which also contributed to the eventual emergence of modern American dramaturgy. One was Jan Kott's exhilarating rethinking of the classics
in his book, *Shakespeare, Our Contemporary*. Kott's legendary work
is credited with sparking Peter Brook's revolutionary stagings of *A
Midsummer Night's Dream* and *King Lear* in England.

As the resident theatres grew in the 1960s and 1970s, the job
profiles of many literary managers were gradually reconfigured to
incorporate a wider range of activities and participation in the pre-
production process, with occasional forays into the rehearsal hall.
In addition, persons with backgrounds as press representatives, critics, directors and playwrights were drawn into critical and advisory roles in the theatres, as the organizations sought ways to improve
their stagings and reach new audiences. On the whole these individuals still functioned in a reactive mode to the work being created, rather than actively participating as collaborators; and most of

the early inroads into the actual rehearsal process were more serendipitous than planned.

Outside the resident theatres there were other growing manifestations of the dramaturgical impulse as well. Arthur Ballet, who created the Office of Advanced Drama Research at the University of Minnesota, was a major catalyst for new play development in the United States. He read more than 12,000 new scripts from 1963 to 1977 and helped initiate and subsidize, with OADR funding, 125 productions, including works by Terrence McNally, Megan Terry, Maria Irene Fornes, Sam Shepard, Rochelle Owens and Jean-Claude van Itallie. Ballet also worked occasionally as a literary manager for the Guthrie Theater and served the national theatre community with his strong advocacy of emerging playwrights.

In 1968 the O'Neill Theater Center established a program for critics, scholars and playwrights to assist other playwrights during the rehearsal period by commenting on the work, suggesting new strategies and leading post-reading discussions. These persons took the title "dramaturg." In the early years, participants included Martin Esslin, Arthur Ballet, John Lahr, Edith Oliver, Ed Bullins and Michael Feingold. This arrangement, instituted during the artistic directorship of Lloyd Richards, continues today. While this was certainly not the first appearance of the title "dramaturg" in the United States, its advent at the O'Neill Theater Center marks one of the earliest popular usages of the word (and its related verb, "to dramaturg"). No doubt the choice of this term, rather than literary manager or advisor, resulted from the desire to distinguish this active rehearsal work from reading scripts, writing press releases or newsletter copy, and editing programs or performing library-bound research.

In the 1970s, several universities added dramaturgy programs to their existing courses of study. These included the University of Massachusetts at Amherst program founded by Virginia Scott; the University of Iowa/Iowa Playwrights Workshop program under the direction of Oscar Brownstein; and the Yale School of Drama program initiated by Robert Brustein. Yale faculty such as Joel Schechter mentored young dramaturgs, instructing them in rehearsal methods and the techniques of creating production casebooks or protocols. Schechter also championed the profession as an editor and writer with articles and whole issues of *Theater* devoted to its theory and practice.

By the late 1970s many literary managers in the regional theatres had changed their titles to "dramaturg." This shift reflected their increasing responsibilities and power in their theatres' hierarchical structures. However, some chose to keep the traditional titles. Even today, in American regional theatre, the literary manager at one theatre may perform tasks nearly identical to those of the dramaturg at another organization, and either of them may execute essentially the same duties as the director of new play development at a third theatre. (Also many dramaturgs still maintain dual careers, such as dramaturg/playwright or dramaturg/critic.)

On occasion dramaturgy has met resistance and has been the source of considerable controversy. Some of us borrowed phrases and attitudes from German and British models, referring to ourselves as "in-house critics," "theoreticians" or "resident intellectuals." We should have been able to predict the reaction from other artists. We fledgling dramaturgs promoted the profession by calling ourselves the "conscience of the theatre" without really knowing what that meant, without anticipating the anti-intellectual strain in theatre circles, nor foreseeing the inevitable cost to our professional reputations of such hubris.

Sometimes the very nature of dramaturgy interfered with its growth. Much of the work done by dramaturgs was behind the scenes and not always properly credited. Since the job profile for the dramaturg has been so multifaceted and has varied so much from theatre to theatre and from project to project, even practicing dramaturgs had difficulty defining succinctly or arguing cogently for the necessity of the profession. This was true in part because so few of us knew anything about the actual work of actors and directors or how to function meaningfully in a rehearsal. Many of the panels at the early conferences sponsored by Theatre Communications Group or the newly formed LMDA were devoted to defining the role of the dramaturg and, in part, to defending the profession's existence. Indeed, an entire issue of *Theater* (Summer/ Fall 1986) was dedicated to this crisis.

Despite the obstacles, over the past ten to fifteen years dramaturgy in the United States has moved beyond the formative advisory and reactive mode of the 1970s to a more collaborative approach. Not only are dramaturgs working more closely with artistic directors in shaping theatres' programming and overall aesthetics, but also many leading dramaturgs are involved in the creation of stage projects from their initial conception through the rehearsal process to the closing night.

Significant pioneering work in the field of production dramaturgy emerged in the 1980s at theatres such as the Eureka Theatre, the Guthrie Theater and South Coast Repertory, to name a few, by dramaturgs who responded to the needs of the project at hand, not through any previously existing theoretical constructs about how they should proceed. They became collaborators in the rehearsal hall, not merely visitors. This metamorphosis has taken them beyond the hidebound traditional definitions of the dramaturg as a researcher and script reader to a role in helping to shape acting, design, directing and textual values, as well as culturally sensitive aesthetic approaches.

In addition to growth within the field, several dramaturgs have chosen to become artistic directors of major theatre organizations, a logical result of the dramaturg's wide-ranging, yet in-depth knowledge of dramatic literature and the theatrical process. A few enterprising dramaturgs have also ventured into opera, dance, film and television, extending the profession into other disciplines.

In any discussion of dramaturgy, the problem eventually arises of attempting to characterize exactly what a dramaturg does on a daily basis both inside and outside the rehearsal hall. Obviously, there is no single answer. It depends on whether the dramaturg is on the artistic staff of a particular theatre, or is a freelancer hired for a specific project. As with any joint effort, the artistic director's or the stage director's willingness to listen is critical: some are eager collaborators and some are not. (Tact, humility and an abiding sense of humor are vital attributes for any practicing dramaturg.)

Whether the production in question involves a brand-new script or whether it is a conventional rendering of a classic can determine the nature of the dramaturg's participation. Then too, since a dramaturg on the artistic staff of a theatre may have a multitude of duties in addition to work on a particular production, the mundane but practical considerations of time and scheduling may have a great impact on how a dramaturg functions. In other words, no single description will be accurate or all-encompassing for every situation. Given that warning, the following reflects my view of the scope of the dramaturg's role, an approach developed largely through my own work at the Guthrie Theater in the 1980s and at Seattle Repertory Theatre and Yale Repertory Theatre in the 1990s.

The primary task for a dramaturg is to aid the artistic director in creating a long-range artistic vision and plan for their theatre, and then to implement short-range actions to accomplish that goal. The dramaturg raises questions about the theatre's mission, particularly in relation to its programming, artists and community. Frequently, the dramaturg must perform an aesthetic high-wire act, for what is often required in interpreting and fulfilling a theatre's mission is both a supportive and a questioning spirit. The dramaturg supervises the commissioning and reading of new plays, cultivating relationships with the playwrights; and rereads the classics, searching for those works that make deep cultural connections. The dramaturg takes the lead in season planning, helping to select plays that fulfill the theatre's commitment to its artists and to its overall vision. Dramaturgs work with directors to challenge fixed notions about new plays or classics being considered for staging. When possible, the dramaturg assists in picking the artistic team for each production and helps to marshal the resources needed to support the artists' approach to the work.

The dramaturg also serves as a resource and active collaborator during the planning stages of a production and throughout the rehearsal period. The production dramaturg is optimally that artist who functions in a multifaceted manner helping the director and other artists to interpret and shape the sociological, textual, acting, directing and design values.

Early in the production process, the dramaturg normally takes the lead or has an active voice in the preparation of the text, which may involve the selection of a translation, the commissioning of a new translation or adaptation, or the decision to use a particular stage version. A dramaturg recommends cuts, both before the rehearsals begin and throughout the process. The dramaturg creates in advance of rehearsal a production casebook that should include, but not be limited to, the following, depending upon whether the project is a new play or a classic: (1) A dramaturg's letter to the director that reflects a wide variety of topics—initial discussions on the text, casting and design; major stylistic and imagistic staging approaches; character interpretations; thematic explorations of past productions; and fundamental questions raised by the act of staging the play in our society today. (2) Pertinent historical, cultural and social background on the play. (3) Significant biographical information on the playwright. (4) Commentary by the playwright in the form of interviews, letters, etc. (5) Relevant criticism or commentary by other artists or critics on the work. (6) A highly selective production history of the play. (7) Images from painters and photographers or other artists, which can complement, challenge and inform the original creative impulse of the director and be of value as well to the actors and designers in their explorations.

The dramaturg should attend rehearsals and previews with regularity so that he or she will know the source of the creative choices. This will inspire "doable" notes or staging solutions and not merely obvious diagnostic commentary. In all areas, the dramaturg should encourage the other collaborators at every opportunity to stay away from reductive impulses and instead to pursue choices that amplify and expose the work's complexity.

Finally, when I am asked to define my most significant activity as a production dramaturg in the rehearsal process I invariably confess, "I question." On every level of my work, whether in production or as a staff member, I strive to be a supportive but questioning force, never an "echo."

The production notebooks in this volume were not commissioned as models for the practice of production dramaturgy, but rather to document and illuminate the creative processes of some of America's most significant theatre artists. But the notebooks do reflect the professional challenges and opportunities of the dramaturg's daily life in theatre. The four production notebooks contained within this book have all been created by practicing dramaturgs: Jim Lewis, formerly of the Guthrie Theater, on *Iphigeneia at Aulis, Agamemnon* and *Electra* ("The Clytemnestra Project"), directed by Garland Wright (1992); Christopher Baker, previously the dramaturg at the Alley Theatre, on *Danton's Death*, directed by Robert Wilson (1992); Shelby Jiggetts, then with the Crossroads Theatre Company, on *The Love Space Demands*, a new performance work by Ntozake Shange (1992); and Paul Walsh, a freelance dramaturg, on *Children of Paradise: Shooting a Dream*, the company-created epic based on Marcel Carné's film *Les Enfants du Paradis* for Theatre de la Jeune Lune (1992–93).

I selected these particular productions for a variety of reasons. It is rare to see a Greek trilogy (particularly one consisting of disparate plays) produced by a contemporary American resident theatre company, and I felt Garland Wright's staging merited attention. Robert Wilson's work is always of import, and made even more fascinating when filtered through the eyes of a dramaturg working on the production. Ntozake Shange's poetic stagings have not been documented sufficiently, and the Crossroads Theatre Company deserves to have its explorations acknowledged as well. Finally, there are only a handful of theatre companies in the United States that create work in a truly collaborative fashion and Theatre de la Jeune Lune's work on *Children of Paradise* is a model we rarely encounter. In all cases, the people involved in these projects are artists of consequence.

At their best, the production notebooks in this volume reflect a "questioning spirit." Peter Stein, the German director, remarked in the interview, "Utopia as the Past Conserved" (*Theater*, Fall 1977), that the "doubting process" was at the core of all their work at the Schaubühne, both in the rehearsal hall and outside it. For Stein's colleague, Dieter Sturm, the legendary German dramaturg, the "doubting process" involves the "destruction of illusionary knowledge (*Scheinwissen*) and the questioning of precipitous analyses. . . ." I hope that one result of the publication of this volume will be an awakening of this "questioning" process. It is my further hope that the notebooks will galvanize future dramaturgs and directors to scrape away the accumulated detritus that generations of faithful "museum" productions have left behind.

The contemporary French writer Hélène Cixous, in her essay "The Last Painting or the Portrait of God," writes about Rembrandt's lifelong struggle to create a revelatory self-portrait. She offers a cautionary admonition to poets and others in their artistic explorations:

> One must have traveled a great deal to discover the obvious. One must have thoroughly rubbed and exhausted one's eyes in order to get rid of the thousands of scales we start with. . . . There are poets who

have strived to do this . . . in quest of what I call the
second innocence, the one that comes after knowing,
the one that no longer knows, the one that knows how
not to know.

The production notebooks in this volume strive to encourage artists to attain the "second innocence."

Ultimately, my hope is that these notebooks will have a long-
term salutary effect on theatre in the Americas by recording the
questioning and the creative solutions used by contemporary artists
to solve production problems. It is my desire that the notebooks
will serve future generations of artists in their explorations of those
innate contradictions, conflicts and tensions which give a play
immediacy, causing it to vibrate for their society as well.

Mark Bly
Project Director and Editor

*Mark Bly is Associate Artistic Director of Yale Repertory Theatre and Co-Chair
of the Playwriting, Dramaturgy and Dramatic Criticism programs at the Yale
School of Drama. His varied professional experience includes dramaturging more
than fifty productions at theatres such as Arena Stage, Washington, D.C.; the
Guthrie Theater, Minneapolis; Seattle Repertory Theatre, Seattle and Yale
Repertory Theatre, New Haven, CT.*

✂✂✂✂✂✂✂✂✂✂✂✂✂✂✂✂✂✂✂✂✂✂✂✂✂✂✂✂✂✂

*Literary Managers and Dramaturgs of the Americas (LMDA) is a professional
association serving literary managers, dramaturgs and other theatre professionals
throughout North and South America. With a job hotline, annual conferences and
various publications, the organization promotes and publicizes the work of its
members and facilitates study and debate on the nature and function of dramaturgy
and literary management in American theatre.*

✂✂✂✂✂✂✂✂✂✂✂✂✂✂✂✂✂✂✂✂✂✂✂✂✂✂✂✂✂✂

"*The* CLYTEMNESTRA PROJECT"

AT THE GUTHRIE THEATER

by Jim Lewis

During the summer of 1992, the Guthrie Theater's Artistic Director, Garland Wright, chose to open his season by retelling the Clytemnestra story. Wright adapted and directed three Greek plays using translations by twentieth-century poets: Euripides' *Iphigeneia at Aulis* (W. S. Merwin and George E. Dimock, Jr.); Aeschylus' *Agamemnon* (Robert Lowell); and Sophocles' *Electra* (Kenneth McLeish). The three plays were presented in two evenings on the Guthrie thrust stage, with *Iphigeneia at Aulis* performed on the first, and *Agamemnon* and *Electra* performed on the second. On weekends, the entire trilogy could be seen in a single day. Jim Lewis, who created this notebook, served as a resident dramaturg at the Guthrie Theater in the early 1990s.

DIRECTOR	Garland Wright
SET DESIGNER	Douglas Stein
COSTUME AND MASK DESIGNER	Susan Hilferty
LIGHTING DESIGNER	Marcus Dilliard
COMPOSER/MUSIC DIRECTOR	Michael Sommers
CHOREOGRAPHER	Marcela Kingman
DRAMATURGS	Jim Lewis, Michael Lupu
VOCAL COACH	Karen M. Kehoe
ASSISTANT DIRECTOR	Anne Justine D'Zmura
STAGE MANAGER	Russell W. Johnson

Iphigeneia at Aulis

AGAMEMNON	Stephen Pelinski
OLD MAN	Richard Ooms
MENELAUS	Stephen Yoakam
FIRST MESSENGER	Peter Thoemke
CLYTEMNESTRA	Isabell Monk
IPHIGENEIA	Kristin Flanders
ACHILLES	Bruce Bohne
SECOND MESSENGER	Richard S. Iglewski
CHORUS LEADER	June Gibbons
CHORUS OF WOMEN OF CHALKIS	Christopher Bayes, John Bottoms, Paul Eckstein, Nathaniel Fuller, Richard Grusin, Shawn Judge, Jacqueline Kim, John Carroll Lynch, William Francis McGuire, Brenda Wehle, James A. Williams
SOLDIERS AND BRIDE'S MAIDS	Scott Comin, Craig Holt, Laura Karpeles, Michael Meredith, Dawn E. Reed, Pamela D. Taylor, Robert Werner, Paul Zemke

Agamemnon

WATCHMAN	John Lewin
CLYTEMNESTRA	Isabell Monk
HERALD	James A. Williams
AGAMEMNON	Stephen Pelinski
CASSANDRA	Shawn Judge
AEGISTHUS	John Carroll Lynch
CHORUS LEADER	Nathaniel Fuller
CHORUS OF OLD MEN OF ARGOS	Christopher Bayes, Bruce Bohne, John Bottoms, June Gibbons, Richard Grusin, Richard S. Iglewski, John Lewin, William Francis McGuire, Richard Ooms, Peter Thoemke, Brenda Wehle, Stephen Yoakam
YOUNG ELECTRA AND CHRYSOTHEMIS	Marguerita Carlin, Amber Zemke
SOLDIERS, HANDMAIDENS AND GUARDS	Richard L. Carriger, Scott Comin, Dawna Fox-Brenton, Craig Holt, Laura Karpeles, Timothy Lee, Greg McDonald, Michael Meredith, Chris Minyard, Ann Ozga, Gena Petrella, Peggy Rassieur, Daniel L. Reed, Dawn E. Reed, Pamela D. Taylor, Jennifer Witters, Robert Werner, Paul Zemke

Electra

ORESTES	Paul Eckstein
OLD MAN	John Bottoms
PYLADES	William Francis McGuire
ELECTRA	Jacqueline Kim
CHRYSOTHEMIS	Kristin Flanders
CLYTEMNESTRA	Isabell Monk
AEGISTHUS	John Carroll Lynch
CHORUS LEADER	Brenda Wehle
CHORUS WOMEN OF ARGOS	Christopher Bayes, Bruce Bohne, Nathaniel Fuller, June Gibbons, Richard Grusin, Richard S. Iglewski, Shawn Judge, Richard Ooms, Peter Thoemke, James A. Williams, Stephen Yoakam
GUARDS AND SERVANT WOMEN	Richard L. Carriger, Scott Comin, Craig Holt, Laura Karpeles, Timothy Lee, Greg McDonald, Michael Meredith, Chris Minyard, Ann Ozga, Peggy Rassieur, Daniel L. Reed, Robert Werner, Paul Zemke

INTRODUCTION

Garland Wright, artistic director of the Guthrie Theater, chose to open his 1992–93 season with a monumental production recounting the tragic Greek story of Clytemnestra. Three plays, each retelling a piece of her saga, would be presented over the course of two evenings: Euripides' *Iphigeneia at Aulis* (translated by W. S. Merwin and George E. Dimock, Jr.); Aeschylus' *Agamemnon* (tr. Robert Lowell); and Sophocles' *Electra* (tr. Kenneth McLeish). On weekends, this five-and-a-half-hour trilogy could be seen in a single day. The entire Guthrie acting company would be involved in the project, which was intended to challenge the company with issues of gender, performance and, ultimately, the meaning of "company" itself.

Set Designer Doug Stein and Costume Designer Susan Hilferty, both long-time collaborators with Garland, would join Guthrie staff members Marcus Dilliard (lighting); Marcela Kingman (choreography); and Michael Lupu and me (dramaturgy) in creating this work. Music would be composed and performed by Michael Sommers. Isabell Monk, the company's leading African-American actress, would play the demanding role of Clytemnestra.

As production dramaturg, my primary task was to research and help choose the texts that would serve as the basis for this project; and in the absence of a playwright, to assist Garland in the editing, shaping and rewriting of the text as the situation demanded, while at all times guarding the integrity of these three very different plays. With the permission and final approval of the three translators (or their estates), we would severely cut large portions of the plays in order to fit them into a two-evening format. In addition, it was my function to provide Garland and all the other participants in this venture with the research and background materials that would make it possible for them to enter into a world so very different and distant from our own.

The final aspect of my participation, and perhaps most difficult to explain, was simply to join in and support others during the incredible journey we had undertaken. We had not set out to create just another play, but instead had ventured in search of the elusive ideal of "company." Success or failure did not depend so much on the final product as on the manner in which we would come together (or not) to assist each other in its creation.

As resident dramaturg at the Guthrie Theater, I was fortunate to be involved with the production from its inception. The following are the events and thoughts I recorded contemporaneously in my notebook. I hope that I have preserved in this format a certain sense of the ebb and flow of excitement, despair, hope and frustration that is inherent in any project of this scope. I personally would like to thank all the participants, especially Garland Wright, for the openness and honesty with which we discussed every aspect of this project while still buried in its midst.

Spring 1991

Garland Wright, artistic director of the Guthrie Theater in Minneapolis, asks Isabell (Izzy) Monk, a member of the Guthrie acting company, if there are any plays she is interested in doing. Izzy remarks that she had been in a production of Ezra Pound's version of Sophocles' *Electra*, in which Nancy Marchand had played Clytemnestra, and that she has always wanted to play the part herself.

Garland is interested in the idea of returning to the Greeks, after directing a production of Euripides' *Medea* the season before (Garland's first Greek play). But his initial reaction is negative. He is hesitant to cast the company's leading African-American actress as a villainess in her first queenly role.

On rereading the play, he confirms his suspicions: Sophocles' *Electra* is an unforgiving play as it regards Clytemnestra. It is, in fact, an incomplete story that only touches on the end of Clytemnestra's life, leaving unexplored the complicated issues that lead up to her murder. As Garland begins looking at the earlier plays, he flirts briefly with the idea of returning to the *Oresteia*, which he had considered doing for the Guthrie's twenty-fifth anniversary season, as a tribute to Tyrone Guthrie's famous production early in the theatre's history. Once again, he decides this is not a good idea, at least not at this time.

Instead, he decides to tell Clytemnestra's complete story by combining *Agamemnon*, the first play of Aeschylus' *Oresteia*, with Sophocles' *Electra*, and to start this new trilogy with Euripides' *Iphigeneia at Aulis*, the first play in which Clytemnestra is actually

Kristin Flanders (Iphigeneia) and Isabell Monk (Clytemnestra) in Iphigeneia at Aulis. *Photograph by Michal Daniel.*

seen as a character. The three plays will be performed as a single five-hour piece, recounting Clytemnestra's entire story: from the moment Agamemnon tricks her into bringing their daughter, Iphigeneia, to Aulis to be sacrificed so that his fleets can sail to Troy; through her revenge upon Agamemnon's triumphant return from Troy; to her death at the hands of her own children.

Garland is personally excited by the challenge of working with the three very different voices of Euripides, Aeschylus and Sophocles. It also gives him the chance to explore more fully the nature of the Greek chorus. In *Medea*, Garland had reduced the chorus to three women, breaking up the text to give them each individual lines. But for these three plays, Garland dreams of a chorus "that can shake the room," comprised of the bulk of the Guthrie acting company.

This is consistent with the Guthrie's larger mission to develop a successful acting company. The men and women of the Guthrie company will not only be required to sing and dance (something many of them are reluctant to do), but more importantly, they will have to learn to confront together the male/female issues that will necessarily arise when men perform as women and women as men.

With issues of gender clearly at the heart of these three plays, "The Clytemnestra Project," as it is preliminarily called, will open the Guthrie's 1992–93 season. Because the main stage will be under reconstruction, the play is to be performed in the Guthrie's Lab, a rough-hewn, open space that Garland thinks will be ideal for this project.

Fall 1991

Garland and I decide that it would be more interesting not to bring in a single translator to unify the three plays; instead we will work on the adaptation ourselves from three existing versions by three different poets. In this way we will maintain the challenge of having three different voices for the three different playwrights.

I gather and read almost all of sixty-plus existing versions of these three plays. The vast majority of the translations read stiffly or feel dated, and are quickly dismissed. Two translations leap off the page as eminently playable: W. S. Merwin and George E. Dimock, Jr.'s *Iphigeneia at Aulis* and Robert Lowell's *Agamemnon*. Although neither is a literal translation, both seem to capture the spirit of the works in a concise, poetic fashion that with editing should play well on stage.

My search to find a suitable Sophocles' *Electra* proves more difficult. The idea of finding a third renowned, contemporary American poet to complete the trilogy is enticing. But Ezra Pound's verse adaptation is just too eccentric for our take on these plays, and none of the versions leap out at us in the same way the first two had. Finally, we settle on a recent translation of the play by the British translator, Kenneth McLeish. We now have the basis from which we will start creating our own new trilogy.

While directing *Marat Sade* on the Guthrie's main stage, Garland takes these three plays and makes a first radical cut. He also adds a speech by Clytemnestra's Ghost (from Aeschylus' *The Eumenides*) to the end of our trilogy to round out Clytemnestra's story.

CLYTEMNESTRA'S GHOST:

>Awake. Women awake. What use are you asleep?
>Because you sleep I go Dishonored among the dead.
>I am driven in disgrace because I dared to kill a husband.
>But I suffered too, horribly, at the hands of my own family.
>Yet no Fury rises for my sake.
>Look at these gashes in my heart.
>Remember where they came from.
>Awaken, you goddesses under the ground

Hear my cries from the grave
A mother betrayed by her husband,
Hated by her daughter, killed by her son. Stand up.
Your slumber and fatigue have dulled the deadly anger
Of the mother-snake. Do not forget my pain.
Arise you Furies, you women—and kill my shame—
Kill my shame.

Winter 1991

Due to budgetary constraints, the reconstruction work on the Guthrie's main stage is postponed. It becomes clear that the only way we can produce such a large project in the coming season is to perform it in two separate parts on alternate evenings on the Guthrie main stage. (A third show, *Private Lives,* will be introduced into the repertory after the two "Clytemnestra" evenings are up and running.)

Garland is reluctant to move the project out of the Lab. He has always envisioned the play performed in front of a large pile of dirt in a corner of this rough, empty space with thirty-foot-high brick walls. The same effect can never be duplicated on the Guthrie's thrust stage with its 1,440-seat auditorium. Similarly, "the heat of these plays would be easier to convey in the Lab." But because of the postponed reconstruction, season planning is behind schedule, and the decision is made to produce "The Clytemnestra Project" in two parts on the Guthrie main stage. Evening one will be Euripides' *Iphigeneia at Aulis*; evening two will be a combination of Aeschylus' *Agamemnon* and Sophocles' *Electra*.

In the ensuing months, the dramaturgical staff at the Guthrie (Michael Lupu, our intern Thomas Kohn and I) gather a wealth of background material, and provide Garland with selected portions of it. The material covers every aspect of the plays: biographical material on the playwrights; historical information about ancient Greece; studies in mythology; scholarly interpretations of the works; slides, photos and relevant artwork; and production histories of various noteworthy productions both produced (e.g. Peter Stein's legendary *Oresteia*) and imagined (e.g. Gordon Craig's sketches and writings for *Electra* and other Greek tragedies which were never staged). Copies of much of this material are also sent to Doug Stein, who will do the sets, and Susan Hilferty, who will do costumes.

Garland reads through everything, but he seems most interested in two items. The first is a book by Loring M. Danforth, entitled *Death Rituals of Rural Greece*. Chapter one is a detailed description of contemporary death and mourning rituals as they are still practiced in rural Greece today. The other is an in-depth study of the film *Iphigenia*, directed by Michael Cacoyannis and starring Irene Papas. We rent a copy of the film for Garland, and even though it is only a very loose version of the play, Garland is greatly taken with it. The harsh, dry landscape and the incessant drumming begin to shape his impressions of the world of the play. It is against this background—of angry/violent men ready to revolt for a lack of wind—that the project begins to unfold.

February 15, 1992

Garland meets for the first time with his collaborators on the project. Both Doug and Susan have been flown in. Also in attendance are: Marcela Kingman, our company's movement coach, who will choreograph the movement; Risa Brainin, the assistant director; and Michael Lupu and I, dramaturgs. Not present are Marcus Dilliard, who will do lights, and Michael Sommers, who will compose and perform the music.

As most of the people present worked on the production of

Medea, references to that play quickly become a shorthand for working together. The chorus "will not be like *Medea*." For one thing, Garland wants to work with masks. Also he envisions a full chorus of between fifteen and eighteen actors. The sets will be simpler, and less filled with elements than *Medea*. Garland sees one basic set for all three locales.

The larger issue is whether these plays are taking place in a "real" place ("like *Medea*"), or rather a non-specific, theatrical world. As opposed to previous productions, Garland notes that he has no precise picture in mind of the world of these plays. Instead, he hears a sound: the sound of metal, like rusty armor creaking, and the silence of a windless world. His vision of Clytemnestra moves over the course of the three plays from a bejeweled, joyful wife/mother to a hollow, armored shell of a woman. He cites the wildly sexual nature of these plays, and especially of the women in them. They are sacrificed or throw their lives away on men, who go about their wars and politics.

Susan feels that the costumes will be "more sophisticated" than *Medea*, but she thinks it is wrong to move the plays to another culture. Doug is originally fascinated by the idea of a void, of erasing the space entirely. The group moves down into the theatre space itself to see if it stimulates any ideas. On the stage is the mat for the Pickle Family Circus, which is performing a two-week run at the Guthrie. At the center of the tumbling mat is a large circle. Garland comments that he finds this idea of a circle, completed by the audience, "interesting."

March 9

Doug presents Garland with a rough model of the set. It consists simply of a slightly raised circle in the center of the stage and a raked "bleacher" in a semi-circle upstage that completes the

The Chorus in Iphigeneia at Aulis. *Photograph by Michal Daniel.*

Guthrie's amphitheatre seating. It is clearly a theatrical space, as opposed to a real or architectural space. Doug explains that the entire design has been created by drawing a series of concentric circles, using a piece of string as the radius. The circles include the audience within the energy of the space.

The question that remains for Doug is: what exactly is the "texture"? He is attracted to the idea of a beautifully polished veneer of black Japanese lacquer for the inner circle, with a series of stones around it. (Doug shows us the lucky stone he always carries with him.) Garland only cautions him not to use Styrofoam for the stones. He wants everything in the space to be real. "The circle should not masquerade as black marble. If it's steel, then it's steel; if wood, then it should be recognized as wood."

Garland is slightly concerned that the set is "too Greek," but Doug is under pressure from the shops to deliver floor plans. They can continue to explore the exact details in the days ahead.

March 24: Workshop, day one

The full twenty-seven-member acting company begins a two-week workshop that proceeds each season. This year's workshop (in light of "The Clytemnestra Project") will focus on issues of gender, and how we as individuals "see" each other. The scholars John S. Wright, from the University of Minnesota's departments of English and Afro-American and African Studies, and Sumitra Mukerji, a graduate student at New York University, are invited in to talk about African and Indian cultures. Both are brought to the Guthrie as part of the Lila Wallace–Reader's Digest Resident Theater Initiative.

The company will also undergo extensive movement training in various Indian and Burmese dance styles. With the assistance of the Asia Society of New York, we have found a series of Burmese dance training exercises to serve as a starting point for our own movement exercises. The object is not for the actors to master the styles in such a brief period. (Burmese men must study the "male" exercises for four years, and women must study the "female" for seven, before they are allowed even to start learning the more complicated dances.) Instead, our intention is to expose the company to a stylized system of gender-specific gestures from which they will develop their own dance vocabulary. The difficulty of the material will, we hope, also bond them together as a group, and make the chorus' work that will follow seem easy by comparison.

March 27: Workshop rehearsal

Garland asks the acting company to read through the first rough cut of the text. He explains to them that although he usually doesn't like to reveal his first "slaughter" draft of a text, he would like to hear the words and get a better sense of the flow of the script. The read-through takes a little over three hours. The brief discussion afterward revolves around the issues of gender that the play raises. As opposed to Aeschylus' *Oresteia*, which returns the focus to the men in its final two parts (*The Libation Bearers* and *The Eumenides*), this trilogy keeps the focus on the women. The men are essentially secondary to the drama of the three plays. They come across as largely vain and out of touch with the general havoc they are causing to the community.

After the actors leave, Garland, Michael and I remain to talk about further changes in the text. Garland expresses a desire to cut the texts even more, especially the chorus in *Agamemnon*. This chorus tends to get sidetracked and digress at length, which detracts from the flow of the plays. Garland remarks how "on-the-surface" these plays seem. Every emotion is stated, the psychology of each character straightforward, leaving nothing hidden or concealed.

Or, as Isabell Monk, the actress playing Clytemnestra, stated in the discussion:

> Most of the time, in realistic acting, you search for the inner motivations of the actions, you even try not to bring feelings to the surface. You want to find out how your characters hide, mask their emotions. With the Greeks though, whatever the characters say, they feel.

We discuss briefly how the plays read a little like the "books" for musicals, clearly missing something without the music and dance. We joke that the ancient Greek audiences may well have looked forward to the "big numbers" that broke up the dramatic action of the smaller scenes.

Garland is also concerned over the fact that Doug Stein will apparently not be around for a number of previews, due to a scheduling conflict. Garland will not have his entire artistic team intact during these crucial days of pulling the pieces together.

March 27–April 6

While the company does movement and choral work in the Lab, Garland, Risa, Michael and I meet on an almost daily basis to finish cutting and polishing the text. We go through the plays line by line, and even word by word, comparing various versions of each speech to make sure that Garland has exactly what he needs for that moment.

Iphigeneia remains pretty much intact, since it will be performed by itself. Euripides' style and sensibility are also the most accessible of the three playwrights' for a contemporary audience.

Aeschylus' style, with its emphasis on choral singing, is the most remote. In *Agamemnon*, we continue to cut large portions of the text. Two of the choral odes are cut almost entirely and another two are combined in order to eliminate any unnecessary "digressions" in the text. Every nonessential line is trimmed from the play. Michael reminds us that the power of Aeschylus' plays lies in their poetry, and in his use of repetition. But in light of our effort to perform it together with *Electra*, we choose the single phrasing which best captures the spirit of that moment and allows us to move the plot forward. By the end of our edits, this nearly two-hour play reads in under forty-five minutes.

Electra also undergoes a strict line-by-line scrutiny. We are tempted to cut even more of Electra's opening lament, which we fear will come across to modern audiences as one long "whine," but decide to leave it more or less intact. It is the sort of thing we can easily cut in rehearsal, or even in previews, when we see how the three plays fit together.

April 7: First rehearsal

The actors are seated around a large table. In front of each is a large portfolio of dramaturgical information that contains: 1) general materials about the plays (including maps, glossaries, genealogies, chronologies, the story of the House of Atreus, a brief history of ancient Greece, and scholarly essays ranging from A. M. Dale's *The Chorus in the Action of Greek Tragedy* to Roland Barthes' *The Greek Theater* to articles on the position of women in ancient Greek society), and 2) specific materials for their individual characters (including versions of their own personal lives and mythologies culled from diverse sources). These materials will serve as a base on which the actors can begin their own dramaturgical search.

Garland confides to the company that his thoughts for these plays did not congeal into a cohesive argument as they usually have in past productions. Instead, Garland confesses that he has returned to some of his basic thinking on *Medea* for the core of his thoughts about all three plays. Specifically, he refers to what he calls our "dark forces":

> I think it's important to remember that the Athenian Greece that we know is mythologized in our consciousness as the beginnings of Western Civilization and the beginnings of sophisticated thought. This was a culture that certainly created the roots for our mathematics, for our ideas about architecture, our ideas about art, our ideas about science, philosophy and certainly lawmaking. But it was in this same culture that citizens were going to ancient priestesses in temples, priestesses who lurked over sulfurous pits and revealed the messages of the gods to its citizens . . .
>
> It is therefore important when one is entering into these plays to be able to speak openly about what I call our "dark forces," and by dark I mean the forces within us that we keep out of the light, the forces hidden, unlit and in the shadows of ourselves. Those are the forces of fear, the forces of anger, the forces of hatred, the forces of murder and the forces of survival.
>
> Prior to civilization's socialization of peoples, these were our natural forces. The process of civilizing is the process of working out systems whereby these forces can be held in abeyance, because these forces also represent chaos, disorder and disharmony, even though they spring from natural instinct. Through hundreds of thousands, perhaps millions of years, we as a species have been genetically bred to unlearn these forces or to be rewarded for denying them.
>
> Leading what is now called the moral life, in relation to these dark forces, is actually a deeply unnat-

Costume sketch by Susan Hilferty for the
Chorus in Iphigeneia at Aulis.

Costume sketch by
Susan Hilferty for Iphigeneia

ural life and a life which our ancestors would have found not only puzzling but extremely dangerous to their well-being. So an understanding of the forces which lead to the *events* in these plays requires us to try to remove from us the layers and layers of shellac of judgments about what is good and what is bad to try to relocate what is natural and what has consequence.

April 8–9: Director's meetings

Garland meets with Susan to discuss her third set of drawings. The costumes are not of any particular period or place, but are drawn from Greek research, adapted to include influences from the Middle East and other cultures that were alive and flourishing at that time. Susan is searching for a "rough and loose" quality that will cut through the essentially pristine nature of Doug's set.

A slow transformation in the colors and quality of the materials will take us through the three different locales and times. In Aulis, Clytemnestra in her jewels and Iphigeneia in white silk will stand in sharp contrast to the men, dressed for war. In Argos, an impoverished chorus of old men awaits the return of their King, while Clytemnestra and her court decadently dress in red silks. And ten years later, after a decade of harsh dictatorship and mourning, the chorus of slave women and Clytemnestra herself are all dressed in black, like nuns in severe distress. Even Clytemnestra's jewels now resemble armor.

✹

Garland meets with Marcela Kingman (movement), Michael Sommers (music), and Karen Miller Kehoe (voice) to discuss the nature of the three choruses. Fourteen different odes by three different choruses will have to be completed in just seven weeks.

Garland speaks generally about the three choruses. All three will enter the stage with a traditional "choregus." Each chorus will be present onstage for the entire play. Although some of the choruses' odes have been heavily cut, still more of the text will be put to music and sung. Exactly how they will be sung or spoken, and the dance or gestures that accompany them, will be developed in separate rehearsal sessions to be run by Marcela, Michael and Karen in rehearsal room 1, while Garland works with the principals in the Lab.

For Garland, the chorus in *Iphigeneia* is the most "slippery." Why did Euripides choose such an unlikely chorus? What could this group of young women, who have come from a neighboring village to see all the soldiers, add to the play?

Dismissing the possibility that Euripides was just mocking the concept of chorus in general, Garland briefly describes how he sees them. They are young girls and their chaperons (to account for the varying sizes and ages of our company). Their bearing is nervous and excitable. They are constantly on the move, afraid to stay still because they might miss something. They will actually sing some of the text, set to music as songs.

Garland sees the chorus in *Agamemnon* more clearly. They are old men, caned, crippled and bitter. They are hardly able to move. They were once "vultures," but have been bent by years of dictatorship. They speak only in a low drone, like the ululating of Zulu tribesmen, or the moaning of the didgeridoo. Their mantra is "Cry death, cry death, but may the good prevail."

In *Electra*, the chorus of old slave women literally crawls and scurries around the stage, trying not to be trampled by the events happening before them. They are constantly working and speak up only when they think it safe. There is the feeling the gods have somehow deserted this place. Garland describes the world as a "fundamentalist" nation that has lost faith in its god.

April 8–13: During the first week of rehearsals

Energy is high, as the company begins table work. The only irony is that Kristin Flanders, the actress playing Iphigeneia and Chrysothemis, is at home with chicken pox. In order not to lose precious time, Steve "Rudy" Bennett (the Guthrie's sound supervisor) has hooked up an odd collection of speaker-phones that will connect Kristin by phone to the Lab, where early rehearsals will be held. All the actors have to speak unusually loudly so that she can hear and take part in the discussion. The company continues to read through the play slowly at the table, stopping to discuss issues as they arise.

Garland asserts that the overall journey of the play is "the decay of a culture seen through the eyes of a family." He then leads the company through a discussion of the major factors they as actors will need to confront in working on these plays.

One of the most difficult to grasp for us today is the Greek religion. Garland reiterates again and again that, as opposed to religions today, the Greek religion was neither a moral system nor a force for morality. It was rather a system of magic, consisting of rituals of purification and appeasement. Remorse and/or regret played no part in this system. Instead, sacrifices were made as an attempt to manipulate the gods in order to gain some sort of advancement. The gods prayed to were also personal gods: gods who had a direct interest in seeing the individual or family prosper. In the end, the question was not one of who is right or who is wrong, but who has the stronger gods, i.e. who "succeeds." The underlying issue is therefore the question of one's personal "fate," as opposed to "free will." Garland leaves the company with a quote from Philip Vellacott, a noted Greek translator and scholar, who cites the "primal" origins of Western Civilization as recorded in *The Aeneid*: "The first word of European culture is ANGER."

✖

After rehearsal, Izzy speaks with anticipation and apprehension about playing the part of Clytemnestra.

> What is intriguing and exciting about playing Clytemnestra is her drive, her passion. I don't mean this in a general way. . . . I mean the sweep of passion between a man and a woman. There cannot be higher stakes than what brings a man and a woman together and what sets them apart.
>
> In my career I've rarely gotten the chance to play anything other than the aunt or a grandmother or perhaps a mother—the kind of person who knows better, is wise, even witty and can give advice to those who are caught in conflict. But with Clytemnestra there is the challenge of being directly and totally engaged in this relationship with Agamemnon—emotionally, sexually, body, soul and mind . . .
>
> The emotions are huge and on display. They are larger than life and carry you on the majestic wings of the spoken verse. The magnitude of emotions such as anger, fear, hatred, revenge, love comes from the passion that drives Clytemnestra in every word and action, no matter how extreme.

During a second day of discussion Garland emphasizes the importance of the music. Music is to be the unifying element of the trilogy. John Lynch, who plays Aegisthus, points out that one theory for the origin of opera was Western Europe's "attempt to recreate what Greek productions might have been." Garland extends the metaphor by reminding the company of the difficulty

Director Garland Wright and Jacqueline Kim (Electra). Photograph by Michal Daniel.

of the task that lies ahead: that we are attempting three different operas by three different composers, probably of different periods. Each chorus must create its own poetry and language; they cannot be allowed to "bleed together" or overlap. In terms of the movement, it means that each chorus must begin by "building a dictionary where there isn't one."

Garland also has words of caution for the principals. They must accept all of the events and details of each play as true for that play, even though they might be contradicted in the other two plays. The discrepancies are to help them each discover how they have changed between plays. More than ten years pass between the plays, and those actors who are in more than one play (especially Isabell Monk) must search for the ways in which his or her character changes, and not merely the ways in which they are similar. He tells the actors that they must all "release" from any attempt to find a realistic sense of time inside the plays, especially *Agamemnon.*

Garland is insistent on not taking the easy way out by trying to simplify the contradictions that these plays present to us in the twentieth century. Clytemnestra has grown to love Agamemnon, despite the fact that he killed her first husband and two children. Agamemnon loves Iphigeneia, and still must sacrifice her. And Iphigeneia is saved by the gods in a miracle—though Clytemnestra may not believe it. The challenge is not to resolve these contradictions, but to embrace them.

Doug presents the company with the final set model. Garland discusses the elemental power of the set, with its concentric circles and ring of stones. Garland has asked friends from all over the world to send him stones, and he calls on the company to do likewise. All the stones are to have a personal meaning, and Garland asks that the actors "tell him the story of each stone." It is a way "to make the space ours." They are to be a constant reminder to the company of the natural forces the Greeks knew to rule their lives.

Doug has made two major changes in the set. First, instead of the outer circle consisting of raised "bleachers," it is a sixteen-foot curved rake that looks like a hill or cupped saucer. And in place of the traditional *skena*, he has hung two simple semi-circles of white starched curtain that extend the concentric circles of the stage up to the rafters. Together they create a strong sense of a horizon. The polished black gloss of the center circle, and white splendor of the curtains give the set an austere elegance, reminiscent of a Japanese tea setting. Garland has his "ritual place that ceremony can take place in." There will be no mistaking this environment for a realistic setting. It is a sacred space in which the actors will perform; the audience is included in this space, invited to observe the action of the plays along with the chorus.

April 14: Second week of rehearsals

After a week at the table, the actors are anxious to get on their feet. Garland begins at the beginning of *Iphigeneia*. Stephen Pelinski (Agamemnon), Richard Ooms (The Old Man) and Steve Yoakam (Menelaus) wander slowly over the Lab floor, getting a feel for the marked-out space. Garland asks them just to read the play on their feet. Agamemnon orders his servant to go and stop Clytemnestra from sending Iphigeneia. But Menelaus, Agamemnon's brother (and Helen's husband), prevents him.

Pelinski and Yoakam quickly become embroiled in the desperation of the scene. No longer "kings," the argument quickly degenerates into a children's angry fight—two brothers each afraid to be seen by the other as weak or "womanly." All pretense of nobility is swept away and, like caged animals, the two brothers wrestle each other to the ground, striking out with abandon. Once separated, Pelinski and Yoakam acknowledge the first discovery of the play: that everyone is on edge, and just beneath the surface is an untold anger.

April 15

Michael Sommers, the composer, is anxious to set up a meeting with Garland. After two days of working with the chorus, he has questions about which way the music should develop. Fascinated by the theatre's new Akai sampler, Sommers can imagine the music becoming quite complicated, with much taping and "bigger-than-life" sounds produced electronically and reproduced with heavy mixing through speakers around the theatre. Or it could go the other way, toward an extremely simple sound with little more than a drum, simple flutes and bells. In the latter, it would be the choruses' voices which become the primary "instruments." All electronic amplification and mixing would be kept to a minimum. The source of "sound" would be the stage.

✻

Garland begins staging the first scenes. Uncharacteristically, he is moving constantly around the three sides of the taped-out thrust stage. Although he doesn't say it, I sense that he is already concerned about how little time he has to do all three plays.

Possibly for the same reason, Garland is spending more time on his feet than is his custom. He frequently interrupts the actors to talk them through various key moments of the scene. Occasionally, he takes the part of one or both of the actors and imagines himself reacting to that moment in the play. The company members watch and then take over, expanding on the kernels Garland has given them.

This scene will repeat itself over and over again for the next seven weeks of rehearsal, as the actions and intentions of the scenes are laid in layer by layer. No actor's choice is totally wrong in Garland's eyes. Every detail added to the complex layering of a performance ultimately gives it its power. Garland's objective is to force the actors to push always further into the complexity of the characters portrayed. The wrestling match between Agamemnon and Menelaus is just the surface of the "primal" anger to be scratched. Every moment and detail of their conflict is to be analyzed and shaped so that all the complexities of their long lives together shade their present crisis. From this one scene, the audience should know both their past and their future.

April 16

The chorus works daily with Marcela, Michael and Karen, while Garland does scene work with the principals. In the first weeks, the

choral work focuses on training the actors to be aware of each
other as part of a group. Exercises in moving in sync, singing in
sync, speaking in sync are repeated over and over in different variations. Energy is focused constantly on the persons next to an individual, not on the individual her/himself. This way of working is
alien to many members of the company, and long stretches of
extremely slow-motion work try their patience. Sometimes tem-
pers flair. Other times the group gets silly. Marcela, Michael and
Karen are often called on to play "cop," a role none of them is eager
to play. At least for the time being, the work is almost entirely
exploratory. The actual text is hardly touched.

Back in the Lab, a plywood mock-up of the set is now in place. The
actors find a new freedom in being able to run up and down the
raked slope. The raised area also adds a new dimension to the space.
Individuals on the risers appear distant, and someone standing on
them becomes smaller than the actors inside the circle. This increases
the impact of the scenes staged within the inner circle. It becomes
a sacred, magical space in which men and women "enact" their
lives. It is a place where larger-than-life passions reign, where des-
tiny takes its course.

　　Garland quickly runs through the opening of *Iphigeneia*,
before moving on. The rough form of these early scenes is already
taking shape. The play opens at an almost unbearably high pitch.
The pounding of drums precedes the scene. It is the voice of the
Greek soldiers crying out for action, raging furies already out of
control. Nothing can stop the tide of events. Agamemnon, in tears,
is a cornered animal. He does not wish to kill his daughter, but the
threat of an angry mob leaves him no alternative. There is *no* noble
choice, only ugly compromise.

　　Actor emotions are equally rough and out of control. Steve
Yoakam (Menelaus) pulls a muscle in his ribcage while wrestling

with Stephen Pelinski (Agamemnon). It is not serious, but serves as a reminder that the passions of the piece need to be carefully choreographed.

Garland spends the rest of the day working on Clytemnestra and Iphigeneia's arrival at Aulis. Even though the chorus is not present, the brief spark of family happiness on their arrival is a welcome glimmer of hope, and relief. It is a momentary calm before the storm of fate washes back over us all.

April 18: End of second week

Chapters from the book *Tragic Ways of Killing a Woman* by Nicole Loraux are distributed to the company. The women are intrigued by her analysis of the ways in which a woman could make a name for herself in an essentially paternalistic society. The ideal of female "glory," to be gained through self-sacrifice, makes a deep impression. They realize that none of the women in these plays is a victim. Their lives are "heroic" in every sense of the term.

The impact of this reading is immediately felt in rehearsal. While sketching out the scene in *Iphigeneia* when Clytemnestra and Iphigeneia make their final desperate appeal to Agamemnon to spare Iphigeneia's life, Garland, in the absence of a baby Orestes, gets down on his hands and knees to portray the baby. Imagining the presence of her baby brother, Kristin Flanders (Iphigeneia) pushes the scene to the emotional edge. Tears flow, as the family rolls and tugs on each other in a true life-and-death struggle. After a short break—"recovery time"—Garland talks at length about the scene. He comments that we could work nine weeks on this scene alone, and cautions the actors that it will be weeks—if ever—before they will be comfortable with it. For the time being, he is not even searching for a physical shape, but rather for a few "emotional anchors" on which to harness the scene.

Garland decides not to stage the final scenes of *Iphigeneia* and jumps to *Agamemnon*, in order to start work on all three plays simultaneously. The search for a different energy begins. We will continue to move around from scene to scene, play to play, to give the colors and layers of this infinitely complex project time to emerge.

April 21

Garland has a long meeting with choreographer Marcela Kingman and composer Michael Sommers. Garland sat in on an evening chorus rehearsal in rehearsal room 1 the night before. He is concerned that they are spending too much time on exercises, and that they have not yet begun to deal with the text. Garland is reluctant to deal with this aspect of the chorus. His hands are already full with the principals, and what little time he will have with the chorus will have to be spent on staging.

April 22

Garland continues to skip around through the three plays (primarily *Iphigeneia* and *Agamemnon*), doing scenes apparently at random. Gradually, Isabell Monk is coming to grips with the complexity of the character of Clytemnestra. Moving beyond the helplessness of Clytemnestra in *Iphigeneia*, today Izzy makes a breakthrough into what she calls the "Cleopatra" inside Clytemnestra. She confesses, "It's always been difficult for me to portray any affection onstage other than maternal. But I like this sexual stuff. And playing to the old men [of the *Agamemnon* chorus], Clytemnestra's a real performer."

Garland shows Izzy a few sexual gestures (pulling slowly at Agamemnon's shirt front before the embrace) but Izzy takes over from there, biting Agamemnon's hand and eventually sucking on his fingers. Izzy laughs off the tension after the scene. "It's very lib-

Chorus from Agamemnon. *Photograph by Michal Daniel.*

erating knowing that [Agamemnon] will be dead in ten minutes. It really helps in getting her juices flowing."

In the next scene Izzy greets John Lynch (Aegisthus) with a hungry embrace over the dead body of Agamemnon. Still holding the murder weapon and covered in blood, Clytemnestra rubs her bloody hands and the weapon over John's chest.

CLYTEMNESTRA:

> The sight of Agamemnon dead breathes
> excitement to my bed.

Garland comments after the scene that the sex between Clytemnestra and Aegisthus that night, rolling in Agamemnon's blood, will be the best of their lives. The link between sex and death in these stories is explicit, as is the characters' essential conflict. These Greeks are not the cool rational people of legend, but a frightening dichotomy of reason and animal instinct. They may strive to be rational, but they are still captives of their animal urges. The "dark forces" Garland spoke of in his introductory talk are finding their way into the play.

April 23

A sacrificial stone altar is placed in the center of the circle for *Agamemnon*; in *Electra*, a sacrificial pig will lay atop it. The memory of Iphigeneia's sacrifice is therefore made a permanent presence onstage for the remaining two plays. It will also serve as Agamemnon's death pedestal and Clytemnestra's deathbed. Human sacrifice is the ongoing curse of the House of Atreus, each death reopening the same wound.

CLYTEMNESTRA:
> The sickness lies so deep in our blood,
>> no man or knife can reach the poison.
> Three times we have washed the stain
>> from our house.
> When the old wound heals, it bleeds again,
>> but I do not pray for death.

April 24

Garland reports having made a breakthrough in the difficult scene in which first Clytemnestra and then Iphigeneia plead with Agamemnon for Iphigeneia's life: "For the first time I saw a layering of emotions, instead of just a single unvarying one."

✳

The chorus work is still going slowly. Although much of the basic movement vocabulary work has been done, only the first ode is finished—and it is still rough.

Marcela Kingman comments on the difference between working with dancers and with actors: "Unlike dancers, the acting company thinks they have to get it right the first time. Today, they got very frustrated and angry. I think by the end of the afternoon rehearsal they learned to use the anger. But they need to learn to relax. The moves and song will come in good time."

April 28

Saule Ryan and Carol Mendelsohn, of the Roy Hart Theatre, which is based in Cevennes, France, are in town for two weeks giving workshops in their specialized vocal training techniques. They have worked with the Guthrie acting company before, and vocal coach Karen Miller Kehoe has invited them back for a day-long workshop aimed especially at helping the company stretch the high and low ranges of their voices, while maintaining the projection they will need on the Guthrie stage. Most of the time is spent showing the male chorus members how to use the upper part of their vocal register to achieve a softer, more rounded sound, rather than a falsetto, to speak the female choruses in *Iphigeneia* and *Electra*.

Michael Sommers, the composer, is excited by the percussion and metal drum that has been made for him by the Guthrie scene shop. Created from a fifty-gallon steel barrel, topped by a horizontal wooden mast and steel mainstays that can be bowed or struck, it looks like it could have been made by the twentieth-century avant-garde composer Harry Partch, from the debris of a shipwreck. The sounds are clearly non-electronic and non-Western, with an eerie, primitive quality, of war drums and tearing armor. "The sounds of the piece," chimes Sommers ecstatically, as he experiments with the different ways he can pluck, bow, strike, beat, shake and scratch the odd-looking contraption.

April 30

Garland asks the chorus to use their masks for the first time as they stumble through the middle section of *Agamemnon*. This is the first step in breaking them of the habit of making small facial gestures and realistic reactions. Garland remarks that they need "to begin to think of their faces as larger than life, and their focus will read larger."

Garland is excited about the look of the masks. All the masks are lightweight neutral half-masks, but each play's masks are finished differently. The *Iphigeneia* chorus masks are gold leaf, shiny and glossy. The *Agamemnon* masks are attached to bald caps and rough, patchy beards. For *Electra* the masks are almost mud caked. "They are like potato-heads, all browns and pocked."

In the evening, the company runs *Agamemnon*. The company is barely ready for this undertaking. Garland has quickly staged the entire play in rough outline so that he can move on to *Electra* and return the chorus to Sommers and Kingman for continued work. As opposed to *Iphigeneia* or *Electra*, there are almost no scenes in *Agamemnon* in which the chorus does not play a major part. In fact, *Agamemnon* is essentially a tragedy about the chorus. Since Agamemnon and Cassandra are relatively minor characters in this play, their deaths can hardly qualify as the makings of great tragedy. It is instead a tragedy of the "polis," i.e., it is the populace of Mycenae whose suffering comprises the tragedy of *Agamemnon*. By the end of the play, they are the helpless victims of near total tyranny—they are the living dead.

The chorus moves are much simpler in *Agamemnon*. As old men, their singing and dancing is held to a minimum. And the men in the company are more comfortable portraying old men rather than young girls in *Iphigeneia*. *Agamemnon* is also (in this production) the shortest of the three plays.

The company does a wonderful job of getting through. Mercifully the play is only sixty-six minutes long.

May 9: First stumble-through of Iphigeneia

Having blocked through most of the three plays, Garland wants to go back and stumble-through *Iphigeneia*. "The scene work depends on the scenes that come before," Garland announces to the assembled company of nervous actors. "Before we can go on, we need to start piecing them together."

After the run Garland talks with Marcela, Michael and Karen about the need to restage the chorus odes (especially the entrance and final exit). The content and meaning of the text is being lost beneath the ornateness of the movement. Garland cites a few specifics in order to give them a better understanding of what he needs. The fact that the chorus is excited by seeing all the Greek ships and soldiers assembled at Aulis is not clear. There is so much movement that we do not hear the text. Nor is the chorus' energy focused outward toward the harbor; instead it is focused inward toward each other and the dance. The final chorus also lacks focus. The text of the ode ("Glory to Artemis") as sung by Kristin Flanders is captivatingly beautiful. But the celebratory dance, in which the chorus circles Iphigeneia and is finally swept away by her determination to sacrifice herself for Greece, goes on too long and fails to build to a dramatic peak.

Garland makes the difficult decision that from now on all the rehearsals will be held with everybody present in the Lab. Despite the shortage of time, he understands that he needs to work more closely directing the chorus, integrating their work into the work

Costume sketch by Susan Hilferty for Clytemnestra in Electra.

he has been doing with the principals. Although he doesn't state it, Garland has clearly determined that he must alter his original vision of the chorus. The chorus will "dance" less; instead, Garland will stage choral interludes that are more pictorial than kinetic. This will leave Marcela and Michael with more time to work on the remaining true dance numbers. It will also give Garland more opportunity to balance the various elements of each play. The chorus must be more attuned to what is actually happening before them, and the principals need to feel the presence of the chorus watching. Both the chorus and the principals need to be aware constantly of the increasing pressure of time and events.

May 12

Garland discovers that he has made a mistake in his original approach to the character of Agamemnon in *Agamemnon*. On his triumphal return from Troy, Agamemnon cannot be a tyrant. Instead, he must return as a politician wishing to restore his country and its government to order and glory. He must be honorable so that his death is a "tragedy." If he is only a villain, his death will not have the necessary impact on either Clytemnestra or the audience. It is the fact that his death is a tragedy that will propel Clytemnestra to her own tragic turn. She is destroyed by finally having achieved what she has so long desired; it leaves her an empty shell whose own death—at the hands of her own children—is yet another in a long line of tragedies.

May 13: Dinner with Garland

During a long dinner with Garland, we discuss how the play is progressing, and how the experience of "The Clytemnestra Project" has been different from previous directing experiences. Garland speaks of his approach to directing in terms of painting. As a director he plays with general "washes of color," "sketching in" moments and details, and finally uses techs to highlight and focus the piece. All of this starts with his very first reading of a play, during which Garland draws certain general impressions. Through research and subsequent readings he gradually develops a more complete overall vision of the play. But things rarely turn out quite as he imagines them. His original vision of the play disappears when rehearsals begin and "never re-emerges until technical rehearsals." Not even during runs does he again see what originally drew him to the piece.

The unique problem that "The Clytemnestra Project" is raising is that the work on each individual scene is going well. But every time we put the scenes together, the "power" of each scene seems to drop out. Garland attributes this to the very structure of the pieces. "These plays are really vaudevilles," he says, citing the basic scene-song-scene-song structures of the plays. Each scene then becomes its own tiny play, and the next scene does not necessarily follow from the scene that came before. The actor's natural instinct to try and carry a character from one scene to the next only undermines what he/she has to do in each individual scene. Garland likens it to Robert Wilson's *The Knee Plays*. Each moment is only about that moment, and the overall work is not held together by a story or an arch, but rather by a series of images, what Garland terms in regard to "The Clytemnestra Project" as "a scrapbook of family photos." Garland's strategy is therefore to work slowly, in order to cement every moment in place, to focus the actors' energies on the drama of each scene and not on a broader arch.

The most difficult play in this respect is *Iphigeneia*, because on first glance it appears to have a plot and through-line. But, Garland insists, the truth is that it has only a situation. Unlike *Medea*, in which Medea makes the decision to kill her children during the course of the play, giving it a dramatic climax, *Iphigeneia* is a play in which the end is a foregone conclusion. No decisions are actually made during the course of the play; instead, the characters (like the chorus and the audience) can only watch as the inevitable chain of events unfolds. *Agamemnon* and *Electra* are similarly structured. All three plays start with a dilemma in which the choices have already been made.

When asked what is holding the individual scenes together, Garland confesses that, at the moment, nothing is holding the scenes together. But if his vision of the play is true, then when each scene "works," the play should hold together like a *prism*—i.e., not by logic of character or situation, but by the beauty of the refracted images. And the most beautiful of these refracted images is the chorus, which in Garland's mind is a unity of music and physical composition.

The choruses are not to be thought of as characters or even as a group; they are not even directly related to the content or argument of the plays. For Garland, they are totally abstract, formal pictures or, as he puts it, the "exquisitely beautiful landscape" of ancient Athens. Their "music" is what can bring these plays to life. They are not just punctuation to the scenes being acted out before them. They are the emotional graph which charts the flow of the play.

Through them, Garland goes on to say, we can get a glimpse of what he terms the "archeology of the theatre." Theatre itself is derived from a choral music tradition that served as the glue for an entire community. And each year that community would reassemble to hear and retouch that music which recalled the very foundations on which their community stood.

All that we have left to us today are a few shards of that poetry. And because we have lost the tradition of "retouching" these shards, of somehow returning to our common past to find the glue which holds a community together, we have lost our ability to "hear" what a community in song is truly like. These plays, these shards of a greater poetry, still offer us a few brief moments in which we can imagine what it must have been like, but we are forever deaf to the true power of these plays. The first run-through has reinforced Garland's original fears about directing Greek tragedy: how to re-instill in an audience today a sense of that original "magic" continues to elude him.

May 19

The issue of time becomes the major concern. Despite Garland's focusing much more of his time on the chorus, the actual movement and vocal work is progressing very slowly. Garland begins to lament the size of the undertaking. "I could do one of these plays in the time remaining; but there is just not enough for all three." Susan Hilferty, who is in town for the duration, echoes these concerns in regard to the overwhelming job of costuming more than thirty actors in three plays. "The problem is that this is not one show, but three different shows. It has all the complexities and problems of three different shows, but we are having to deal with them as if they were one."

Garland is also facing another possibly irreconcilable problem. The idea of casting all three choruses out of our company is undermining the chorus in *Iphigeneia*. Although they are trying their hardest, the actors are having difficulties finding the correct energy for these young girls. Ideally they should all be contemporaries of Iphigeneia. They are young girls who must share in the excitement of her arrival and empathize with the horror she feels at the unthinkable turn of events. They must feel with Iphigeneia the weight of the nation demanding her death and then be swept away by the "glory" of her decision to sacrifice herself for the greater good of Greece.

Although they themselves play no part in any of this, the chorus is the window through which the audience can view the horror of the events tearing Iphigeneia's young life apart. They should be nothing more than children before the gods, tiny in relation to the size of the events churning in front of them. But with most of them played by men, many of whom are over six feet tall and weighing in at nearly two hundred pounds, the chorus tends to diminish rather than accentuate the impact of the events taking place before them.

May 22

Garland observes after a much improved run-through of *Iphigeneia* that he is unsure of how the audience will respond to the play.

> Our difficulty in dealing with *Iphigeneia* is due to our inability in this age to handle "generosity," to accept the very idea of giving ourselves to someone or something larger than us. Iphigeneia's self-sacrifice is almost incomprehensible to us. *Agamemnon* and *Electra* are much easier for us to grasp because they are about revenge, something still very much a part of our psyche.

The issue is compounded by a recurring problem Garland has faced working with the classics the last ten years. All of his classical directing has been centered around trying to prevent the reduction of characters to people "just like us." Garland points out that, as opposed to Chekhov, who writes about immediately recognizable characters, the Greeks (and Shakespeare) deal in an "iconography of royalty" that suffers when it is reduced to being "about us."

This is not just a by-product of method acting. It is a larger national, cultural phenomenon which denies the existence of

"Great Ones"—a group of individuals (once kings and heroes and even gods) through whom we could see enacted great moral and existential struggles. It has reached such an extreme in contemporary society that we cannot even sight the "Great Ones" anymore; they have all been reduced through over-exposure, scandal sheets and such to people just like us. Possibly, Garland muses, it is the legacy of capitalism or democracy or even the placing of man instead of God at the center of the universe—"a very inelegant portrait of our universe."

These plays demand that an audience believes in "heroes," and believes in its own intimate relationship to "the gods," i.e., fate. When Kristin Flanders (Iphigeneia) raises up her frail arm to heaven and sings out the words "Glory to Artemis" in a voice far too big for her small body, or Jacqueline Kim (Electra) screams her agony out to the world at an unrelenting pitch, these are moments intended to force us to re-examine what it means to be a part of something larger. For it was, and still is, the primary function of these plays to bring a community together and to help them reach a consensus about what are and what are not valid "rules" by which a community acts and governs itself.

In fact, Garland is now feeling the lack of Aeschylus' *Eumenides*, the final play in *The Oresteia*. It is in this play that the endless revenge cycle that has destroyed the House of Atreus is finally put to rest before the first public trial. The desire to close out this horrible chapter in human history (whether actual or purely mythical) is incredibly strong. Having spent the last ten weeks opening ourselves up on a daily basis to the "dark forces" has been a draining ordeal, and we crave resolution. Garland is keeping up a good front, but the whole experience is taking its toll.

✶

Garland and I discuss the problems that became apparent in this afternoon's run of *Iphigeneia* and *Agamemnon* back to back. No mat

Costume sketch by Susan Hilferty for Agamemnon.

ter how hard Garland works to bring out the personal cost of Iphigeneia's death for Agamemnon, Agamemnon comes across as simply a villain. We only judge his behavior in terms of his violation of paternal trust. But these plays are not simply about Agamemnon killing his daughter and getting killed in return. They also involve issues of community and "duty." The true tragedy of his position is the necessity that his great office imposes on him. Either he can be a great leader or he can save his daughter.

Garland is concerned that if we cannot in some way empathize with Agamemnon's "tragedy," we will never be able to appreciate the complexity of Electra and Clytemnestra's dilemma in *Electra*. Our desire to see everything in terms of good and evil, right and wrong, obscures the true "tragedy" of this family caught up in a cycle of violence.

Only tonight's run-through of *Electra* will tell us if Garland's concerns are justified. Despite his concerns for the general context in which *Agamemnon* will be received, he is fairly happy with the overall shape of the piece. *Iphigeneia* is another matter. There is still a great deal of work to be done, especially in terms of incorporating the chorus. If *Electra* is likewise in need of a great deal of work, Garland fears there won't be time to make major changes in two plays.

※

The run-through of *Electra* is better than expected. But the unspoken opinion of most of the parties involved is that there is not enough time to address all of the problems that exist. The difficult question arises of what is worth spending precious time on, and what should just be sacrificed.

May 25–28: The first three days of tech

The first moment of tech is frighteningly beautiful. Eight pin spotlights make the stones placed symmetrically around the black ring glow ominously. The question is how the actors will fare in this cold, inhuman space.

Garland is upset ("suicidal") over the coldness of the space. The shock of moving from the rough, earthy Lab to this austere, black-and-white set is unsettling for all. What appeared to be an empty, flexible space in the model now calls out for a very different sort of play than the one we have been working on for the last seven weeks. Fierce emotions and base passions seem lost in this sterile setting. And the stark white curtains upstage set off every gesture in a harsh light. The world created by the set calls for opera; even the most powerful of performances will seem muted.

The first problem to address is the breaking up of the white curtains. Garland asks if the curtains could be gold or amber to add some warmth to the space, but Doug informs him that the material cannot be dyed. Doug suggests that a gold border along the bottom might give the curtains a more tapestry-like quality. A gold strip of material is quickly found and pinned across the bottom of one of the curtains. Garland then experiments with raising a number of the curtains part way, thereby giving them a more architectural look. Though not totally satisfied with the results, Garland decides that they can continue to play with these changes as they move ahead.

Costumes are also posing some problems. Most have an earthy, worn texture consistent with the work. But many feel like "costumes" and heighten the operatic quality of the play's look. Susan is struggling under the burden. She reminds us that this is really three plays, not one, and that the demands of doing three entirely different sets of costumes are overwhelming.

The masks, too, are altered by the space, and seem somewhat out of place. Rather than ancient, they read almost futuristic in this austere Japanese-lacquer setting. The elements are coming together oddly, in ways no one intended. There is a cacophony of styles and textures.

The techs are further slowed by what can only be the angry gods. The Lighting Designer, Marcus Dilliard, is pulled away from his work when his wife goes into labor five weeks early.

The actors are also not coming together as we might have wished. The bonding which never seemed to occur during rehearsals continues to elude us. The chorus especially seems to lack cohesion and, worse, seems to lack the will to work toward such an end. There is no rebellion, as such, but the theatre is missing a sense of energy. Excitement about the plays is not palpable.

Although Garland keeps up a good facade for the most part, he too is showing signs of exhaustion. The overwhelming task of trying to pull together three floundering plays has taken its toll. The first day he is extremely testy. By day two he has regained his composure, but jokingly asks if it might be possible to just perform *Agamemnon* and *Electra*. On day three—without a lighting designer and with progress going slowly on the set changes and costumes—Garland moves ahead by dismissing altogether the idea that he is teching the shows. Instead, he works on restaging a number of scenes in *Electra* under a single, constant light cue. The question is: will Garland have the strength to confront the myriad of problems that now show so glaringly in the harsh environment of tech?

May 30

The absence of the Lighting Designer Marcus Dilliard (because of the premature birth of his baby girl) has accidentally given *Electra* its look. Having worked on the set with a constant, unchanging wash of white light, Garland finds it apropos for the sensibility of the play. *Electra* will be played in an dreary, pale-white glow: an airless, prestorm heat suffocating all who live in repressive Argos.

The oppressive lighting pushes the actors to new extremes. As if to mock Clytemnestra's smearing herself with Agamemnon's blood, Jacqueline Kim (Electra) takes what she thinks to be her brother Orestes' ashes from the urn and smears her own face and hair with them. The moment is a horrifying twist on the House of Atreus' bloody wounds. With Orestes gone, Electra thinks her hopes of revenge are ended. There will be no more blood, just a living death.

ELECTRA:

> O ashes of Orestes, dust of the dearest of men!
> Dear ashes, where are all the hopes
> I had when I sent you away?
> You were a torch of hope for all our house,
> And now you are nothing, dust in my hands.
>
> Oh my darling,
> My dearest darling,
> O Orestes, take me with you
> Nothing to nothing, inside the grave;
> Let me lie with you forever.
> We shared everything, you and I.
> Let me share your death! There in the world below
> Pain ends, and sorrow ends. The dead are at peace.

Garland and Doug have made a breakthrough on the set. Once again, an accident dictates the turn of events. By chance, Doug wanders into the space while our Technical Director, Ray Forton, is removing a center portion of the raked slope to repair an element beneath the set. Doug is so excited by this new configuration that he immediately seeks out Garland. Together they pursue the possibilities . . .

For both *Agamemnon* and *Electra* the center of the raked slope will be removed, creating a ramp entrance upstage center. The white curtains above the opening will be fully raised to create what appears like a massive doorway into an unseen palace. Pillars will be placed on each side of the opening, giving the entire space the feel of a large temple in which these plays are being performed. It is from this portal that Clytemnestra's servants will unroll the red silk tapestries on which Agamemnon will march unknowingly to his death. The opening will also frame Clytemnestra's bloody re-entry with the bodies of Agamemnon and Cassandra.

Costume sketches by Susan Hilferty
for the Chorus in Electra.

This accidental discovery has drastically altered the look of the three plays, clearly distinguishing Aulis' becalmed shores from Argos' troubled palace. It has also served to break up the massive operatic feel of the space. The actors are no longer dwarfed by the setting. There is now a greater sense of perspective and dimension, and for the first time since moving on to the main stage the action of the play seems to fit the space.

I show Doug and Garland the sketch by Gordon Craig for a production of *Electra* which was never staged. In it a large doorway in a curvilinear space frames a tortured Electra. It is a space that very much resembles our own. The sketch is accompanied by a quote from Craig which reads:

> A vast and forbidding doorway, I often think, still remains the best background for any tragedy . . .
>
> *On the Art of the Theater,* p. xvi.

I remind Doug and Garland that this was the very first item that I had given them over six months previously. We have a good laugh at the idea that the image has been lying in our subconsciouses all this time.

The new spatial arrangement, however, means that Garland will once again have to restage a number of crucial moments. Possibly the one we will all miss most is Jacqueline Kim's wonderful first entrance as Electra. In the Lab, from the upstage center rake, she entered crawling backwards, relentlessly bemoaning her fate—a woman so destroyed by her personal anguish that she literally could not see where her agony was taking her. But now with the center ramp gone, this scene, as well as a number of others, is restaged. This particular moment will never be as powerful as it was in the Lab, but the transformation of the space is creating a much more positive feeling all around. Suddenly, everyone seems inspired.

A feeling that we just might be able to accomplish all of the changes necessary has raised everyone's spirits. With costumes advancing well, and work being done on the masks to make them more appropriate, it remains to be seen only how much can be accomplished in the remaining four days of tech. Even though the *Electra* tech promises to be relatively simple, no actual light cues have even been written. Similarly *Agamemnon* is not yet complete, and Garland—in order to not cheat *Electra* of necessary rehearsal time—has never even staged the final two scenes of *Iphigeneia*. It is possible that we may not be able to run some or all of the plays before the first preview.

This possibility terrifies Garland. The performances are still so fragile that he is concerned about the company's reaction to possibly harsh criticism from audience members and friends. Despite the improved mood, the company as a whole is very insecure about these plays; a negative audience response might tear the already weak unity of the company totally apart.

June 5 and Beyond: Previews through opening

On the afternoon of June 5 we have a wonderful final run-through of *Iphigeneia*. Garland has urged the company and especially the chorus toward a simplicity of motion that lifts the focus of their performances to a new high. Kristin Flanders, as Iphigeneia, is especially focused, and her difficult transition—in which she chooses to embrace her death—comes as close to carrying us with her as it has ever come. It is only at the moment that she says, "If only one man can see the sunlight/what are the lives of a thousand women in the balance," that we are pulled from the play and her "sacrifice" trivialized.

At dinner, prior to the first preview, Garland, Doug and I discuss cutting these lines. Garland is energized. For the first time in a long time, he has been reconfronted with the complexity of ideas broached by this play.

He is also invigorated by having once again rediscovered the wonderful structure of *Iphigeneia*. Each main figure is given his/her moment to express his/her case. First, Agamemnon is shown in his dilemma, having to decide whether or not to go ahead with his own daughter's sacrifice. Next Clytemnestra is caught up in it, having been tricked into bringing her daughter to her own death, and she now turns to a stranger (Achilles) to beg for help. And last, Iphigeneia herself begs to be spared.

Euripides then thrusts all three protagonists together (in what would have been a relatively new dramaturgical innovation at that time) to let them fight over the resolution. The simplicity of the structure and the complexity of the issues create a dramatic powder keg. To succeed, the actors must give themselves over to this "simplicity," thereby allowing the large issues to come out—to try and do too much or push too hard buries the plays.

For Garland it is ultimately the issue of Iphigeneia's self-sacrifice for something larger than herself (i.e., for Greece) which most captures his imagination. In the words of Achilles, it is Iphigeneia's ability to "reconcile what should be with what must be" that becomes the cornerstone of all three plays.

This is why it is so vital that the audience be carried away with Iphigeneia and her decision to die for Greece. In Ariane Mnouchkine's version of *Iphigeneia* (which I had seen the previous fall in Paris, but Garland had not seen), the play is transformed into a virulent antiwar statement in which Iphigeneia and the entire chorus get caught up in a wave of nationalist, moblike furor. In contrast, Garland sees in Iphigeneia's death a truly heroic act of self-sacrifice. But he again questions whether in this day and age we can still appreciate, or even begin to contemplate, the complexities of such an act. (In jest, Garland muses on how such ambiguity can be "marketed.")

The discussion returns to the question of whether to cut Iphigeneia's lines unfavorably equating the value of a thousand women's deaths to the life of a single man. Whether or not Euripides meant this ironically, a contemporary audience cannot hear this line without being reminded of the debate over sexual equality. But as important a topic as this is, and as central as the gender issue is to the entirety and conception of "The Clytemnestra Project," coming at this moment in the play, these lines actually undercut the impact of *Iphigeneia*.

In a strange way it lets the audience off the hook. The complexity of Iphigeneia's self-sacrifice becomes trivialized in light of her comment about the worth of women. Although we are somewhat reluctant to cut these "telling" lines, we decide to do so. [*Note*: The lines, however, remain in large print on a page in the program dealing with the role of women in ancient Greece. It is too late to change the program, and the discrepancy will lead to a number of heated post-play discussions with audience members.]

Now in previews, Garland once again becomes philosophical about his function as a director. He talks about having learned to "give over," and cites gardening as having been instrumental in teaching him this lesson. As a gardener, you learn there are only so many things over which you truly have control. You can prepare the soil, and you can try to insure the quality of the seed. But once you've planted, there is really very little you can do but watch and hope the seeds take root, and gently nurture the few plants which actually begin to grow. Then there are all the outside factors over which you have no control at all: animals, bugs, frost, too much or too little rain, too much or too little sun, and all of the other variables which determine how your garden grows. The same is true in the theatre. As much as any director tries to prepare for all of the unexpected factors that will arise, ultimately there is only so much of a production over which the director has control. The rest lies in the hands of the gods.

Agamemnon and *Electra* preview on June 6. After the first previews of all three plays, it becomes clear that it is *Agamemnon* and *Electra* that will require most of the time remaining. *Iphigeneia*, though somewhat of a letdown after the strength of the afternoon run, holds up relatively well in front of an audience. The basic structure is there, and we are quite pleased with its shape for a first preview. What remains to be done is focusing and tightening the detail work, and allowing the actors to grow into their parts.

The performance of *Agamemnon* and *Electra*, on the other hand, reveals some fairly significant dramaturgical and structural flaws. Nevertheless, Garland is pleased by how well the actors performed their work; it is now clear to him what he has to do.

Foremost in his mind is the need to "orchestrate" *Agamemnon* and *Electra* into a single evening. Although we have always treated them as separate plays, Garland now realizes that the audience views them as acts one and two of a single play. (Once again the decision not to do all three plays as a single play or as three entirely different plays comes back to haunt us.)

The implications are manifold. *Agamemnon*, especially from the moment of Agamemnon's murder to the end, must not be allowed to have a sense of closure. It must drive forward and set up the events that are to follow in *Electra*. Garland has been working on establishing Clytemnestra's victory as a Pyrrhic one: that having achieved what she dreamt of for ten years, she is left with nothing to live for. But now, Garland realizes, *Agamemnon* must end with Clytemnestra in a state of exultation, rejoicing in her revenge.

Similarly, Aegisthus must sweep through the end of the play, elated at his "victory." To revive an image Garland used when talking about the moment months before (and then forgot): "Clytemnestra and Aegisthus are exiting to the greatest sex of their lives, in the blood of Agamemnon." By trying to anticipate Clytemnestra's transition into *Electra*, Garland had inadvertently undercut the impact of *Electra*.

Sophocles' *Electra* also poses a serious structural problem for us in the context of a combined evening. In Euripides' version of this same story, the dramatic tension of the play is maintained by allowing the audience to believe Orestes is dead. But in Sophocles' version, the audience knows from the opening scene that Orestes has returned. Consequently, Electra's suffering does not affect us in the same way as if we, too, believed her to be in a helpless situation.

Equally problematic is the fact that the play ends with Orestes rejoicing in the murder of his mother. Although we know he will be pursued by the Furies, no mention of them is made in Sophocles' version. And even if we sympathize with the character of Electra, it is hard to feel for Orestes, who in this version is little more than a cipher. The addition of Clytemnestra's Ghost speech from *The Eumenides* helps resolve Clytemnestra's story, but essentially the trilogy—as we have constructed it—ends on an unresolved note.

There is a great deal of discussion about cutting the opening scene of *Electra* altogether. It is not essential to the plot of the story, and it might well make Electra a more sympathetic figure. But to cut it would turn Orestes into nothing more than a plot device and make the ending of our trilogy even more ambiguous. It also seems a violation of the text. Although we have heavily cut much of the original plays, we still feel that we have been "loyal" to the spirit of the pieces. To cut the entire opening scene of *Electra* would be to make Sophocles' play something that it isn't. We will have to find another alternative.

Garland thinks he can at least partially solve the problem by downplaying the opening scene of *Electra*, while heightening other elements that will help make the audience forget Orestes. But exactly how we will end the trilogy still eludes us. Clytemnestra's Ghost speech may be cut entirely or trimmed back radically. It once again seems like an appropriate end, but it might just be another "easy way off the hook" for both us and the audience. Its obvious feminist message seems to give us a way to avoid having to face the complexity of these plays straight on.

The question of how the three plays finally do fit together

Shawn Judge (Cassandra) in Agamemnon. *Photograph by Michal Daniel.*

does not conform to any easy, formulaic answers. It is a complex journey from a young woman's oddly heroic self-sacrifice to her sister's insatiable need to achieve her own personal sense of justice. And these two "fanatical" acts are merely the frame for what can only be seen as the destruction of a woman and the deterioration of a family and a society (polis).

On the eve of the opening, every possible ending seems to leave us elusively short of where these powerful plays want to take us. It is possible that the attempt to produce these three pieces together—any one of which is severely challenging to bring to life on the stage today—was an act of hubris that defies our ability to reach a satisfying sense of closure.

Winter 1992

The sense of having tried to bite off more than we could chew stays with us through opening night and for the duration of the plays' three-month run. The production garners a great deal of attention both locally and nationally, but the feeling of "if only" remains. Garland leaves for a well-deserved sabbatical having sworn never to do another Greek play. But four months after his departure, I get a postcard from Athens. On it is a picture of the Acropolis, and once again Garland is musing what it must have been like to see these ancient tragedies staged there.

Jim Lewis has worked as a Resident Dramaturg at the Guthrie Theater, Minneapolis; Second Stage Theatre, New York City and INTAR Hispanic American Arts Center, New York City. His adaptations include Chronicle of a Death Foretold: Dangerous Games *on Broadway and* Tango Apasionado *Off-Broadway (both with Graciela Daniele). He also has served as Director of Performing Arts at the American Center in Paris, France, and is currently work- ing in New York on a new production with Bill T. Jones.*

S E L E C T   B I B L I O G R A P H Y

Aeschylus. *Agamemnon*. In *The Oresteia of Aeschylus*. Translated by
    Robert Lowell. New York: Farrar, Straus and Giroux, 1978.

Aristotle. *Poetics*. Translated by Gerald Else. Ann Arbor: University of
    Michigan Press, 1967.

Arnott, Peter D. *Public and Performance in the Greek Theater*. New York:
    Routledge, 1989.

Baldry, H. C. *The Greek Tragic Theatre*. London: Chatto and Windus,
    1971.

Barthes, Roland. *The Responsibility of Forms: Critical Essays on Music, Art,
    and Representation*. Translated by Richard Howard. New York: Hill
    and Wang, 1985.

Beauvoir, Simone de. *The Second Sex*. Translated and edited by H. M.
    Parshley. New York: Alfred A. Knopf, Inc., 1952.

Boardman, John, et al., editors. *The Oxford History of the Classical World*.
    New York: Oxford University Press, 1986.

Bowra, Cecil M. *The Greek Experience*. New York: Praeger Publishers, 1969.

Cameron, Averil and Amélie Kuhrt, editors. *Images of Women in
    Antiquity*. Detroit: Wayne State University Press, 1983.

Craig, Edward Gordon. *On the Art of the Theater*. Boston: Small,
    Maynard, and Company, 1911.

Eisler, Riane. *The Chalice and the Blade: Our History, Our Future*. New York:
    Harper and Row, 1987.

Euripides. *Iphigeneia at Aulis*. Translated by W. S. Merwin and George E.
    Dimock, Jr. New York: Oxford University Press, Inc., 1978.

Girard, Rene. *Violence and the Sacred*. Translated by Patrick Gregory.
    Baltimore: The Johns Hopkins University Press, 1972.

Grant, Michael. *The Classical Greeks.* New York: Charles Scribner's Sons, 1989.

Graves, Robert. *Greek Myths.* 2 volumes. New York: Penguin Books, Inc., 1955.

Iphigenia. Motion picture based on Euripides' *Iphigenia at Aulis.* Director: Michael Cacoyannis. Cast: Irene Papas. 1977.

Keuls, Eva C. *The Reign of the Phallus: Sexual Politics in Ancient Athens.* New York: Harper and Row, 1985.

Kitto, H. D. F. *Greek Tragedy: A Literary Study.* New York: Methuen, 1961.

Loraux, Nicole. *Tragic Ways of Killing a Woman.* Translated by Anthony Forster. Cambridge, MA: Harvard University Press, 1987.

Millet, Kate. *Sexual Politics.* New York: Doubleday, 1970.

Paglia, Camille, *Sexual Personae: Art and Decadence from Nefertiti to Emily Dickinson.* New Haven: Yale University Press, 1990.

Pomeroy, Sarah. *Goddesses, Whores, Wives, and Slaves: Women in Classical Antiquity.* New York: Schocken Books, Inc., 1975.

Segal, Erich, editor. *Greek Tragedy: Modern Essays in Criticism.* New York: Harper & Row Publishers, 1983.

Slater, Philip E. *The Glory of Hera: Greek Mythology and the Greek Family.* New York: Beacon Press, 1968.

Sophocles. *Electra, Antigone, Philoctetes.* Translated by Kenneth McLeish. New York: Cambridge University Press, 1979.

Vellacott, Philip. *Ironic Drama: A Study of Euripides' Method and Meaning.* New York: Cambridge University Press, 1975.

Walton, J. Michael. *The Greek Sense of Theatre.* New York: Cambridge University Press, 1984.

Webster, T. B. L. *Greek Theater Production.* London: Methuen, 1956.

Wood, Michael. *In Search of the Trojan War.* New York: Penguin, 1985.

Zimmerman, Bernhard. *Greek Tragedy: An Introduction.* Translated by Thomas Marier. Baltimore: The Johns Hopkins University Press, 1991.

Bibliography compiled by Belinda Westmaas for the Guthrie Theater study guide to "The Clytemnestra Project."

$\mathcal{D}$ANTON'S DEATH

AT ALLEY THEATRE

by Christopher Baker

In the election year of 1992, Robert Wilson returned to his home state of Texas to stage *Danton's Death*, Georg Büchner's epic tale of the French Revolution. The extended production process was divided into three phases over an eight-month period, a rarity in American theatre. This Alley Theatre production opened in the fall of 1992 in Houston, employing Robert Auletta's new translation. The production notebook that follows was created by the then-Resident Dramaturg, Christopher Baker.

NEW ENGLISH VERSION BY	Robert Auletta
PRODUCTION CONCEIVED AND DIRECTED BY	Robert Wilson
SCENIC DESIGN	Robert Wilson
COSTUME DESIGN	John Conklin
LIGHTING DESIGN	Stephen Strawbridge and Robert Wilson
ASSISTANT DIRECTOR	Ann-Christin Rommen
MUSIC	Chuck Winkler
SOUND DESIGN	Joe Pino
MAKEUP DESIGN	Debra Coleman
PRODUCTION STAGE MANAGER	Tree O'Halloran
DRAMATURG	Christopher Baker
CO-PRODUCER	Michael Wilson

CAST

DANTON	Richard Thomas
JULIE	Marissa Chibas
HERAULT–SECHELLES	John Feltch
ADELAIDE	Jennifer Arisco
ROSALIE	Emily York
WOMAN	Gage Tarrant
SECOND WOMAN	Katherine Pew
CAMILLE	Scott Rabinowitz
PHILLIPEAU	Jamie Callahan
MAN ON THE STREET	James Black
ROBESPIERRE	Lou Liberatore
LEGENDRE	Willis Sparks
LACROIX	Jeffrey Bean
MARION	Annalee Jefferies
ST. JUST	Jon David Weigand
FIRST GENTLEMAN	Thomas Derrah
SECOND GENTLEMAN	Wade Mylius
LUCILLE	Melissa Bowen
HERMAN	Peter Webster
THOMAS PAINE	Gregory Boyd
JAILER	Bettye Fitzpatrick
FOUQUIER	Thomas Derrah
WARDER	James Black
BOY	Jason Miesse
CARTER	James Black
EXECUTIONER	Bettye Fitzpatrick
CITIZENS	Peter Baquet, Glenn Dickerson, Matthew Rippy

Danton's Death, written in five feverish weeks in 1835, was the twenty-one-year-old Georg Büchner's first play. It is possibly, as Büchner translator Carl Richard Mueller suggests, "the finest first play ever written." Fragmentary and seemingly plotless, the play depicts the disintegration of revolutionary ideals into a bloody struggle for power in the latter days of the French Revolution. The fanatical and pious Maximilien Robespierre has risen to power and instigated a Reign of Terror on "enemies of the Revolution." Georges Danton, self-styled libertine and great orator of the Revolution, opposes him. He calls, after so much bloodshed, for moderation. Fanaticism, however, abhors moderation, and Danton is imprisoned and executed.

The drama focuses on Danton in existential crisis, unable to believe in the possibility of human contact, unable to justify his past actions and unwilling to flee his own destruction. Yet, after all hope of rebellion or escape is gone, Danton launches a glorious attack on tyranny itself, using as artillery his oratorical genius and powerful voice in one last, futile attempt to change the course of history.

The proposition of matching Büchner's cynical, passionate descant to the crystal imagery of theatrical wizard Robert Wilson came about in the spring of 1991. Wilson's production of Ibsen's *When We Dead Awaken*, produced by the Alley Theatre in collaboration with the American Repertory Theatre, was opening in Houston. Alley Artistic Director Gregory Boyd invited Wilson to

become an associate artist of the Alley Theatre and to create several
pieces over a five-year period.

Ticket sales for *When We Dead Awaken* were exceeding
expectations, and upcoming presentations of Wilson's work at the
Contemporary Arts Museum and the Houston Grand Opera were
already generating interest from avant-garde aficionados and the
newly curious. Given the enthusiasm both in the artistic institutions and in the community, Houston seemed the right place for
Wilson to establish another artistic base.

For his first project, Wilson chose a play he had seen several
times in Europe and had been thinking of staging for some time—
Danton's Death. He was particularly interested in making an American
production of a play rarely performed in the United States.

In 1992, a year of politics and social upheaval, *Danton's Death*
seemed a fortuitous choice. That Robert Wilson would be staging
this German masterpiece in his native state, Texas, and not in
Germany, where his productions are more abundant, added to its
attraction.

The project also posed many challenges. *Danton's Death* is
heavy in text, and derives much of its power and meaning from
rhetorical subtleties and logical argumentation, things for which
Wilson's work is not known. And one wonders what Büchner,
who railed against the cold-bloodedness and marionette characters
of "idealistic" dramatists (Schiller in particular), would make of
Wilson's cool, formal style.

Yet, in one way, Büchner and Wilson are alike: neither is
interested in resolutions or pat morals. Büchner's personal sympa-
thies are certainly with Danton (he drew on his own letters for
some of Danton's speeches), but his political views are more in line
with the reformist Robespierre. Wilson is drawn to Büchner's play
because, he says, it "has no conclusion." Both prefer the paradoxical, the unresolved, the unanswered.

Wilson and Boyd asked the *When We Dead Awaken* creative

Annalee Jefferies (Marion) and Richard Thomas (Danton) in Act II, Scene 4.
Photograph by T. Charles Erickson.

team—Designers John Conklin and Stephen Strawbridge and Assistant Director Ann-Christin Rommen—to join the project. The production was set for October, 1992.

As dramaturg at the Alley, I became involved early in the process. This production notebook gives some indication not only of the day-to-day decision making, but also, I hope, of how each step is part of an overall structure that Wilson has developed to create his unique productions. Wilson's strategy of creation is structure—of light, of movement, of space, of time and of the rehearsal process itself. The Alley Theatre, the actors, the designers and technicians all adjusted to this extended and new (for most) way of working.

Wilson divides the process into three phases, which, for *Danton's Death*, were spread over eight months. Each phase has clear objectives and requirements:

Phase A. Design Conferences. These took place in February and April. Wilson created the "visual book" of the play, scene-by-scene sketches, which would serve as the framework for the production. During this time, preliminary decisions were made about the adaptation and casting.

Phase B. Workshop and *Bauprobe*. Lasting most of June, this phase brought together a company of actors to work with Wilson in order to generate and set basic choreography or blocking for the entire piece. The blocking was meticulously recorded and served as the basis for the work in the final phase. At the end of the three-week workshop, the Alley's Large Stage was cleared, and a full-scale mock-up of the set was installed for the *Bauprobe* or "scenic rehearsal." This day-long event allowed logistical problems to be solved before any scenic elements were built.

Phase C. Rehearsals and Technical Rehearsals. The final phase included a five-week rehearsal period leading up to the previews and opening. These rehearsals began September 22.

In between the phases (and during them as well) Wilson

worked on other projects, often traveling to other cities. He sees these not as disparate jobs, however, but as parts of one body of work; parts that affect, and are affected by, the works before and after them—a continuum.

The separate phases serve a twofold purpose. First, it is an economical and efficient way to tackle a large-scale project, since all decisions are given time, and scenic elements can be tested in the workshop and *Bauprobe*. Actors can learn blocking quickly in Phase B, and so are able to come to Phase C prepared.

Apart from economy, however, the extended rehearsal period gives everyone time, Wilson says, to live with the work. "Only after you've lived with it can you understand it."

Compared to other productions, this process seems backwards: we begin with what we see and hear, and then make "sense" of what has been created. Motivations or meanings are rarely discussed—Wilson relies on the actors to create those on their own. Rejecting hermeneutics, he creates the physical production, scenic and kinesthetic, separately from the text. The traditional hierarchy of theatrical elements (the primacy of the verbal) is rejected. A discussion between Wilson and the actors during the workshop is typical: his first question, "How is Danton's relationship with Marion different from his relationship with Julie?" is followed by "How are you dressed?" Character and costume are addressed at the same time and with equal importance.

Though a well-planned, intelligent process, it was primarily non-intellectual. Though rigidly predictable in structure, rehearsals were often improvisational and explorational. It was, for this dramaturg, quite literally an eye-opening experience, requiring keen visual and aural sensitivity, more than analytical or critical faculties. I sometimes felt that I was perceiving problems in the piece because I was thinking too linearly or conventionally. Other times I wondered if the "unconventional" nature of the process kept us from addressing issues we probably should have considered.

My work, aside from that of chronicler, centered primarily on matters of the text: working closely with adapter Robert Auletta, serving as his proxy in rehearsals, and helping to shape, through daily adjustments, the performance text. Wilson spent little time analyzing or discussing specific textual changes. Instead he outlined his general approach to the words, and relied on others to fulfill those intentions. It is for this reason that the people who work with Wilson—actors, assistants, designers, etc.—are so important to the process. They are expected to be thinking, revising and improving the piece, more or less autonomously, and then to bring these discoveries to the rehearsal hall, where they can be tested and either incorporated or rejected.

I would have liked it if my role had included much more input into matters beyond textual concerns and historical research. I wonder how a dramaturg might function better in this process. Is there anything that the dramaturg, specifically, can contribute to the choreography sessions or *Bauprobe* that any other informed observer could not? How does one go about dramaturging a dance? Can one dramaturg a sculpture?

Wilson relies heavily on his collaborators, but as the predominate creative force of the project, his personality and temperament shaped the mood of rehearsals and meetings. Though I hope this chronicle captures his great artistry and intuitive abilities, it does little to reveal his constant charm and unique sense of humor, accompanied by an unlikely and infectious laugh.

PHASE A: DESIGN CONFERENCES

February 2, 1992

First meeting. Gregory Boyd, Associate Director Michael Wilson and I are joined by Robert Wilson, Assistant Director Ann-Christin Rommen, John Conklin (who will design costumes and co-design, with Wilson, the set), and Stephen Strawbridge (who will co-design the lighting). Gregory Boyd has prepared an edited version of the play to use in these conferences. Other members of the Alley staff have been recruited to help read the text. I have compiled historical research, critical articles, biographical information on Büchner and a guide to events of the Revolution. In addition, I have made a schematic diagram of the play that is put up on the wall and serves as a visual reference to the many scenes of the play.

Wilson has obviously done some thinking about the play and the Alley stage before this meeting, but these sessions are a chance for Wilson to respond intuitively to the spoken text. With little discussion beforehand, we begin to read the play aloud. Wilson listens, following along in his text. Afterwards, we go into the theatre to look at the Alley's Large Stage, an oddly shaped thrust featuring two sets of six-foot-high cement "bunkers" as entranceways that jut onto the stage, and a set of walls—also cement—which act as a proscenium arch far upstage.

Wilson talks generally about the space he envisions: a sparse, mostly black area, in which actors are isolated by light. For the end

Phase A design conference with John Conklin, who designed the costumes and co-designed the sets. Photograph by Jim Caldwell.

of the play, in which Danton and his associates are executed, Wilson imagines the entire stage becoming very, very white.

February 3–4

Wilson has in front of him many sheets of white paper and at least two dozen pencils. As we read the play aloud again, Wilson makes sketches of what the stage will look like during each scene. He labels the paper with Büchner's epithet for that scene: a street, a room, the Tribunal, etc. On some of the drawings he makes notes, clarifying what each element is or does.

After each scene we stop reading and Wilson explains the newly completed sketch, describing each element and how it might move or function. John Conklin tries to get some ideas of the textures, colors, materials, etc., that Wilson envisions, and himself offers suggestions on how the scenery might be executed. Our

comments and questions on these sketches are general, and somewhat tentative, as we try to move from Büchner's linguistic construction to Wilson's spatial one. Some of the questions Wilson
cannot answer: he is finding his way as well.

This method of creation serves Wilson in several ways. By
reading the play aloud, and getting immediate feedback from the
group, Wilson is able to respond to the overall structure of the text
more spontaneously than he would reading and analyzing it himself. It also allows him to consider the play as a spoken, rather than
written, text from the very beginning.

When finished, the drawings create a large storyboard of the
entire production. As Wilson explains, "Once I know what a space
looks like, it's easier for me to make decisions as to what to do."
Wilson calls these sketches the "visual book"—a spatial, architec-
tonic and largely abstract rendering of the play. A structure of light
and dark, shape, silhouette, recurring visual themes and movement,
it serves as the basis of all work to follow. It is the first indication
of how the set should look and function, how light defines and
reshapes the space and where actors are positioned.

In Wilson's drawings, the back of the stage works like an iris,
able to create rectangular openings of any dimension at any point
in the plane of the proscenium. It allows for some scenes to be
played against the lighted cyclorama and others against blackness.
It allows an opening to move across the stage or to gradually get
smaller until it disappears.

For I-1, which takes place in a drawing room (a brothel?),
Wilson has drawn a black space with two figures downstage left.
Inspired by Büchner's indication of a card table, there is a white
square center stage. For I-2, Büchner writes simply "The Street."
Wilson's sketch shows a path of light cutting across the black stage.
When Robespierre enters the scene to address the citizens, he
appears in silhouette in an opening as tall as the proscenium, the
top of which guillotines down toward him until he, at the last

moment, steps out of its path while the panel continues moving to the floor.

The crowded, noisy Jacobin Club is rendered as a dark, empty space with a single podium standing like an obelisk center stage. In I-4, the prostitute, Marion, reclines on what looks like a white chaise; it is labeled "A Marble Sofa." In I-5, the only meeting between Danton and Robespierre, the latter sits, Marat-like, in a copper bathtub, a burning rope dangling from above. Shapes and visual motifs repeat themselves; the path of light that was the first street comes back in different variations for other street scenes. Wilson also finds surprises to break expectation. In one prison scene a Romantic landscape is visible in the background. ("*That* will be a surprise," Wilson says.) In another, a black panther (!) prowls upstage. In the last scenes of the play, the stage becomes completely white, both floor and cyclorama, with a column of cold, white fluorescent light representing the guillotine.

Production Manager Nina Chwast tapes the sketches to the wall, arranged by act. The visual design of the production is before us. Joined by Technical Director Tony Bish, we discuss the realization of the drawings into actual scenery. Though there will undoubtedly be changes between now and September, we expect the basic elements to remain the same. The plan will be to construct a full-stage square deck, 28' x 28', that is one foot above the permanent stage floor and is covered in charcoal gray, low-pile carpet. Two hard-edged horizontal curtains and top and bottom roll drops will create shutters on either side of the proscenium. Behind those will be a scrim, a rear projection screen and the permanent white cyclorama. The color palette will be primarily black and white. "Very rich, dark blacks that are full of color, sometimes against cold whites, or iridescent whites or opalescent whites," explains Wilson.

We look at paintings of the period, mostly of Jacques-Louis David. Wilson is drawn to the stillness of the portraits, the attention to detail and the cool, porcelain tones of the faces and hands.

Artistic Director Gregory Boyd (right) discusses Wilson's sketches with adapter Robert Auletta. Photograph by Jim Caldwell.

David will serve as the model for both the costumes and makeup. Wilson and John Conklin agree that the costumes should suggest early nineteenth century, very carefully tailored. Wilson would like some of the costumes to have the colors of "jewels"—beautiful greens or reds—that stand out against the black and white of the scenery.

By the third day John has made a three-dimensional model of the set and we talk through each scene again, experimenting with the model shutter system, pointing out the possibilities of each configuration. John has found a Caspar David Friedrich painting he thinks can be a prototype for the prison landscape. We also discuss the possibility of projecting Brechtian scene titles on the sides of the theatre.

We turn our attention to the text. Clearly the developing production is sparse, featuring isolated characters and moments instead of historical pageantry, and we all agree that Büchner's text, which took three and a half hours to read, needs to be shortened. Our goal is to focus on the essential material (the essence), and to cut away much of what places the play in a specific historical time and place. The adaptation should have the fewest possible characters onstage at one time, especially in what are traditionally the most crowded scenes, and be understandable to a modern American audience.

The "street scenes" are particularly challenging. Using Shakespeare as a model, Büchner parodies these Revolutionary heroes with the bawdy humor of the common citizens, who call for more bread in their bellies and more blood in the *Place de la Revolution*. How to render these without falling into a caricature of Shakespeare-cum-Büchner peasants and without the entire population of Paris cluttering up the stage?

One intriguing idea: the street scenes become monologues, comic turns or even songs performed by one or a few actors. (There is precedent for this. Max Reinhardt tried to use one actor to capture the "essence" of the common Parisians.) Wilson likes the idea of undercutting the seriousness of a play with "Death" in the title, and we try to think of these scenes as "knee plays"—Wilson's term for *entre acts* or connective scenes that are unrelated to the plot but are thematically linked to, or comment on, the production. In *When We Dead Awaken*, the onus was lifted from the title by knee-play numbers written by the vaudevillian Charles "Honi" Coles. Here, instead of adding scenes, we try to work within Büchner's dramaturgy.

We discuss at length the three main women in the play, Julie, Lucille and Marion. The question is raised as to whether or not the three women could be played by the same actress, but this seems to make too much of a comment, too interpretive. It also would rob these three unique roles of their power. We are all drawn to the prostitute, Marion. Though her one scene (I-4) is not essential to the plot, her amoral story of sexual insatiateness and death is the most haunting and poetic writing of the play.

March 1992

In between conference sessions, Alley Resident Sound Designer Joe Pino joins the process. Wilson, meanwhile, listens to tapes of composers to provide songs for the street scenes and underscoring for the entire production.

Playwright Robert Auletta is asked to do the adaptation. His successful adaptation of Euripides' *Ajax* for director Peter Sellars makes him a logical choice for this particular pairing of an aggressive directorial hand and classic text, and his own playwriting style seems suited to creating an American, "essential" version of Büchner's play.

I send Auletta the research and my notes from the February meetings. We talk about various ways to cut half of Büchner's thirty characters, eliminate confusing historical references and delete some of the red herrings that appear late in the play. Auletta begins this formidable task immediately; the adaptation needs to be completed by the June 6 workshop.

April 24–26

Conferences continue with more detailed discussions about the physical production, and we continue to talk through the play using the model. Wilson makes adjustments on a few sketches. Some questions have already been answered (though we located a black panther, city ordinance prevents us from using it in the production), and new ones come up (how and by whom will the marble sofa be constructed?).

In a meeting with Bob Auletta and me, Wilson explains that he would like to retain as much of the formal, rhetorical quality of the text as possible. He is interested in the long speeches, especially of Danton:

> I see the speeches as big blocks of arguments that have rather hard edges sitting in opposition to one another. There's a certain tension in the presentation of these ideas very carefully placed together. I see this text being presented to the audience in a very clear, straightforward manner. Words that are bitten rather coolly, and the passion is in the coolness. . . . With *Danton's Death* I'm especially curious about how the play actually has no conclusion; it's something that one can think about long after the play is finished. In fact, the play doesn't finish. Somehow we have to pose the various questions that can be as relevant today as they were two hundred years ago.

Before leaving, Wilson auditions the Alley's resident acting company. In each audition, Wilson performs an improvised, minute-long movement sequence that he asks each actor to recreate as best he/she can. Wilson is looking for actors who move well, but also for those who can *see* movement. He then asks them to read Robespierre's Act I speech stirring the Jacobins to action. Invariably, the actors are emotional and fiery, and Wilson asks them to color the speech less, to be more matter-of-fact. "This pencil is yellow," he demonstrates. "It sits on top of a white piece of paper that is on top of the table. I want a hamburger with ketchup, pickles, lettuce and mustard. Very simple. Matter-of-fact." He coaches the actor to connect the ideas, thinking of the speech as one continuous line, rather than a series of phrases. The auditions go well, but Danton, Robespierre and St. Just are not cast in Houston.

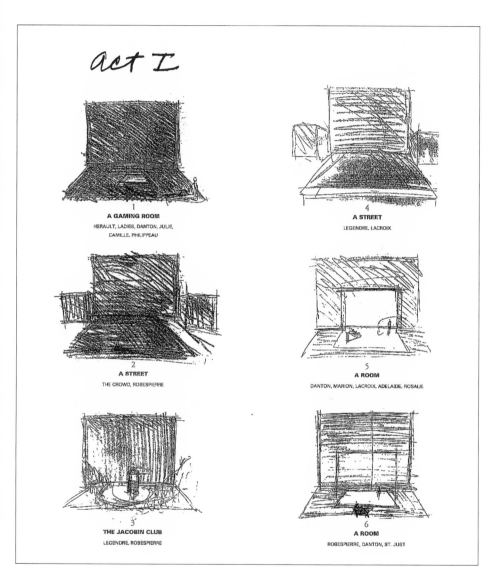

Robert Wilson's storyboard sketches made during Phase A design conferences.

Act II

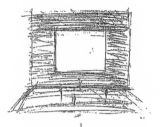

1
A ROOM
DANTON, LACROIX, PHILIPPEAU, CAMILLE

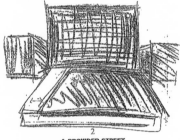

2
A CROWDED STREET
BEGGAR, GENTLEMEN, ROSALIE, ADELAIDE,
DANTON, CAMILLE

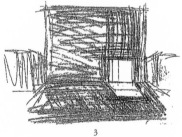

3
A ROOM
DANTON, CAMILLE, LUCILLE

4
AN OPEN FIELD
DANTON, MARION

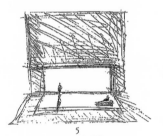

5
A ROOM, NIGHT
DANTON, JULIE

6
A STREET
CITIZENS, DANTON

Act III

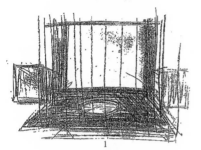

1
PRISON
LACROIX, PAINE, HERAULT, DANTON, PHILIPPEAU,
CAMILLE, JAILER

4
THE PRISON
LACROIX, CAMILLE, DANTON, PHILIPPEAU, HERAULT

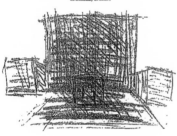

2
A ROOM
FOUQUIER, HERMAN

5
A ROOM
HERMAN, ST. JUST, FOUQUIER, WARDER

3
THE REVOLUTIONARY TRIBUNAL
HERMAN, DANTON

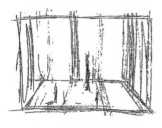

6
THE REVOLUTIONARY TRIBUNAL
DANTON, FOUQUIER, CAMILLE, HERMAN

act IV

1
A ROOM
JULIE, A BOY

2
THE PRISON
LACROIX, HERAULT, DANTON, CAMILLE, PHILIPPEAU

3
OUTSIDE THE PRISON
JAILER, A CARTER, LADIES, LUCILLE, CAMILLE

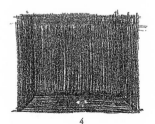

4
THE PRISON
DANTON, CAMILLE, LACROIX, HERAULT,
PHILIPPEAU, JAILER

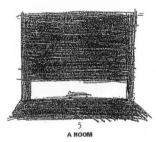

5
A ROOM
JULIE

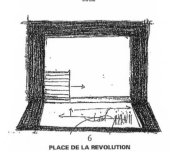

6
PLACE DE LA REVOLUTION
LADIES, A BOY, HERAULT, CAMILLE, DANTON, LACROIX, PHILIPPEAU,
A CARTER, EXECUTIONER

May–June 1992

All departments of the theatre begin to prepare for *Danton's Death*, which will clearly be the centerpiece of the upcoming season. Especially for the technical departments, this will be the most challenging production the Alley has attempted. Though *When We Dead Awaken* originated at ART, it gave us a model of how to plan both time and resources. The 1992–93 season has been arranged so that no production will be playing in our smaller Arena Stage while *Danton's Death* is rehearsing or performing. All energy will be focused on this project. ("If anything," Production Manager Nina Chwast says later, "we were overprepared.")

Casting continues in New York. Lou Liberatore is cast as Robespierre and Richard Thomas as Danton. Wilson likes that Richard has dance training and is not the large, unkempt, bull of a man that one expects in the role.

At the theatre, mock-ups are made of all the furniture and set pieces, except the shutter. The first act of Bob Auletta's adaptation arrives in May. It is much shorter than the original, but little of what Auletta cut is missed. Stage Manager Tree O'Halloran and Houston Composer Chuck Winkler join the production.

PHASE B: WORKSHOP AND *BAUPROBE*

June 9

First day of the workshop. On one wall of the rehearsal room hang Wilson's scene-by-scene sketches. Across from them, photocopies of David portraits: *Madame Récamier, Monsieur Sériziat* and others.

After the cast and staff members introduce themselves, Wilson quickly goes through his sketches, explaining the scenic elements, costumes and makeup.

Full-scale mock-ups, of wood and cardboard, fill the halls on either side of the rehearsal room. In one corner sits an impressive configuration of sound equipment: a Kurzweil keyboard, two samplers, a multi-effects processor, a digital audio tape (DAT) recorder, and cassette and reel-to-reel tape players. These allow Chuck Winkler and Joe Pino to develop the sound score in rehearsals, working with Wilson and the actors from the beginning. Against one wall is a video camera, which will be used to record Wilson's demonstrations of movement and to document the final run-through.

Wilson gives some brief remarks, introducing the cast to his ideas of a formal theatre:

> I'm not interested in naturalism. I hate naturalism. To act natural is a lie. We can be more honest saying something is artificial. . . . Formalism means a distance from what one is saying or doing. In distance, one has more respect for the audience. I prefer not to impose, but let the audience enter the stage at will, on their own. We're there to make suggestions, but not to insist. . . . I think what we see is what we see and what we hear is what we hear, and frequently for me in the theatre it's difficult to do both of those things simultaneously. What I've tried to do in the theatre is to set up a space where a text can be heard and where what we see can reinforce what we hear, but doesn't always have to be subservient or a decoration or an afterthought to what we hear. . . . I do the visual book first, so the movements, the things one sees onstage are not usually illustrative. They don't necessarily follow the text. It is like a radio play and a silent movie. In a radio play there is mental space where one can imagine what things might look like. In a silent movie there is mental space for one to imagine the sounds. Everything is not dic-

tated. Somehow the attempt is to do both of these at once. If we think of the text and the visual book separately, like a radio play and a silent movie running simultaneously, we can create a piece that makes one listen *and* watch. It leaves more space for the audience to imagine.

Though Bob Auletta has pared down the text to almost half its original length, Wilson admits to the cast that this play is nonetheless daunting. "It's a lot of text," he says. "It makes me nervous to do it."

On break, Wilson meets with Ann-Christin, Michael Wilson and me in an office set up for him just outside the rehearsal hall, complete with facsimile machine and CD player. On the walls are sketches from this and other projects, reminders of people to contact, and a picture postcard of Marlene Dietrich. Wilson's appointments, phone calls, meetings and work sessions are dutifully organized by Rodney Cuellar, Wilson's personal assistant in Houston.

We look at the drawing of the first scene and discuss where people are in the space, where they come from, what kind of space it is (public, private, etc.) and what the scene establishes. Wilson looks for a simple headline for each scene—a short, encapsulating description. This will be his method of preparation before working on a scene. I give Rodney a list of headlines for each scene, which he writes on the appropriate sketch hanging in Wilson's office. Before rehearsing a scene, Wilson consults the drawings and meets with Ann-Christin or Rodney to figure out what the text requires. He notes the entrances and exits, and writes down some ideas for movement patterns. He also plans how long each scene will be, in minutes and seconds, and approximately how many moves should happen in that time. Armed with these parameters, Wilson allows himself the freedom to use improvisation and intuition to create the choreography for each scene.

The actors read I-1. "We have to discover the line of development, the overall line of the piece," explains Wilson. "Think in headlines for each scene. What is being said. Simply. Theatre is about one thing first, then it can be about many things. We find the line first," he makes a strong line with his arm, hand and finger pointing into space, "then we can . . . ," his voice trails off, his finger tracing a curving, twisting line in the air. "Then we can make it something else."

He begins to choreograph the scene. As in the sketch, Richard, as Danton, is placed downstage left with his head in the lap of Marissa Chibas, who plays his wife, Julie. Upstage, actor John Feltch as Herault plays cards with two prostitutes, as indicated by Büchner. A white cardboard square, resting on top of the reclining prostitutes, serves as a table. The ladies spill out from the sides to play cards and tease Herault.

Wilson asks the actors to improvise the first part of the scene without lines. Tree and Ann-Christin write down the movements the actors create. Their notations are very specific: the turn of a head, the angle of a foot, the quality of a gesture. Wilson stops the improvisation halfway into the scene and tells them to "think in lines. It's okay to do something abstract, without meaning, not related to the text. . . . Think about it formally—drawing in space. Don't know what you are going to do next."

The actors improvise again, this time more abstractly, as if in a modern dance piece. The new movements are recorded and numbered. Wilson leaves the hall to allow the actors time to recreate the movements they have just generated and to learn each movement's corresponding number. When Wilson returns, the scene is reviewed again. Ann-Christin calls out the numbers and the actors execute the appropriate movements. From here on out, everything created in the workshop will be meticulously recorded and numbered in this way.

Wilson makes adjustments, putting the playing cards in the

June 12

We begin I-3, in which Robespierre moves through the angry crowd in the Jacobin Club to deliver his first oration of the play. Robespierre will be alone; the speeches of the other Jacobins are to be recorded and used as part of an opening sound collage. Chuck and Joe develop a score that culminates in a hard blowing wind.

Center stage is a podium, several ladder rungs leading to the top. Wilson demonstrates a movement pattern, a large spiral pattern that ends downstage of the podium, moving as if in some crowded house of horrors, his body distorted by the forces that push him through. Liberatore recreates Wilson's choreography, accompanied by the sound score, and moves to the top of the podium. Wilson then talks Liberatore through a series of thirty-five very isolated, specific moves: "Pick up your right hand, make your hand very flat. Bring your right hand up. Stop. Make a fist with your right hand. Bring your right hand under your left hand. . . ." The moves are numbered, and Lou reviews the gestures. Later the movements are put together with the text, in the same way that I-1 was developed.

This (with the one exception of I-2, the first street scene) is the method Wilson will use throughout Phase B. Each scene's choreography is generated, numbered and learned. It is then paired with the text. The actors then substitute textual cues for numbers. This combination of structure and chance results in scenes that appear to have their own laws of nature and behavior. The experience is of a performance in code, and I am reminded of the semaphoric gestures found in Renaissance religious paintings. One wishes a view from far above the actors were possible, to discern the movement patterns and changes of spatial relationships. Sometimes, despite all efforts to the contrary, one even discerns flashes of psychologically justifiable behavior.

June 13–14

Much of the work in these two days focuses on technique: ways of walking; how to turn in one, smooth, uninterrupted movement; putting more space around gestures; and how to enter the stage in a neutral, utilitarian manner.

Although very little focus has been given to speech or line readings, Deborah Kinghorn holds sessions with the actors to help them with a cold, clear manner of speaking, thinking of the text in long, sustained lines, rather than in short phrases.

Scene I-4. The confrontation between Danton and Robespierre. The scene is in three parts. Lou (Robespierre) is in the bathtub mock-up. This will be the only time Danton and Robespierre share the stage, and Wilson does not want the movements to distract from the ideas. He choreographs a simple pattern that incorporates much stillness, but as the actions are paired with the text, Wilson finds he has miscalculated and runs out of moves long before the text is finished. He starts over, and, indeed, the new pairing focuses one's attention on the exposition of two very different philosophies of life and politics, on Danton's Epicureanism and Robespierre's "virtue."

Continuing with the second part of the scene, Wilson uses the video camera to tape himself creating choreography for St. Just, who is still not cast. His movements are like those of a tormented angel slowly attempting to take wing.

In the final section, Robespierre is alone. He rises from the tub and delivers a reflective speech about the pain of his lonely crusade of divinely inspired terror. The sound is harsh—wind and a metallic, industrial sound. It builds to a crescendo and then abruptly cuts off, leaving him in silence. Wilson blocks him far upstage, arms outstretched in crucifixion, slowly turning. "I am alone," he says, a grotesque Christ figure, struggling with internal demons in the desert. The image is one of the most startling and beautiful yet to be created in the workshop. Afterwards, Wilson turns to the table, and, as usual, asks, "Is this okay?"

June 15

Wilson auditions Jon David Weigand for St. Just. He is concerned Jon David looks too similar to the other actors, but likes the way he moves. Jon David will join the cast tomorrow.

June 16

Wilson, Joe and Chuck review a sound vocabulary to be used throughout the workshop. Working from a list Wilson made in the interim, they create a library of sounds: a nail file, glass breaking, paper tearing, nuts cracking, a music box, water dripping, water running, fire crackling, a calliope, wind, drum rolls, quiet explosions, orders shouted in the distance, ocean wave, wolves howling, gunshots and a cannon. Joe is able to have many variations of each sound available, which in turn can be further processed and layered during rehearsals. This vocabulary is a helpful tool, not only in narrowing the universe of possible sounds from which to choose, but also in creating a certain sound "palette" for the production.

Wilson stages II-2, the second street scene, in which Camille and Danton walk among soldiers, prostitutes and a pair of theatre-going gentlemen, in a parody of bourgeois revolutionaries. (In a speech that has been cut, a father agrees to name his new son "Pike Marat," so as to be the pinnacle of Revolutionary correctness.) We decide to try the earlier idea of setting the scene to music, and I contact Bob Auletta about turning this dialogue into song lyrics.

Scene II-4. Annalee Jefferies has asked if her character, Marion, can appear in the scene. Büchner's text indicates Danton is alone in a field, fighting memories of the September Massacres, "flirting with death." Previously, Wilson encouraged the actors to give suggestions of different ways their characters should be rendered, including places in which characters can appear, even if their appearance is not indicated in Büchner's text.

Wilson thinks Marion could be seen in a different plane than Danton, upstage of the proscenium, as if we are seeing two spaces or times simultaneously. Finding a bolt of white cloth in the costume shop, Wilson creates a seductive and haunting dance for Marion, moving across the back of the stage, enshrouding himself in the unrolling bolt of cloth, which is held taut by an offstage crew member.

June 19

During a break, Wilson, John Conklin, Nina Chwast and Properties Manager Jennifer Young look at a new mock-up of the bed for II-5. It will be a black upholstered chaise, whose shape resembles the curved side of a grand piano, turned on its side. Serving as a headrest is an inset crystal ball. The rehearsal mock-up is made of painted plywood, with a ball of paper, and later a large light bulb, as the headrest. Though a rehearsal piece, it has been built as close to specifications as possible, so that adjustments can be made before the actual furniture piece is built. Conklin uses tape and black cardboard to make small adjustments to the shape.

Great care is taken in making these adjustments. Often, the decisions involve a few centimeters, half a centimeter. The furniture and other objects are not only set pieces to be manipulated by actors for the brief run of a production, but also art objects, with a "life" of their own, on view both in and out of the production. Some will end up in galleries, some may find their ways into future exhibitions of Wilson's work, some even into other productions.

Charcoal drawing by Robert Wilson, 1992, titled Danton's Death, *Act II, Scene 1. Photograph by Art Industrial.*

Wilson concerns himself with both functions: the way in which it will work as a set piece ("She'll have to lay too far down... the crystal ball will hit her in the back... she'll slide off. ...") and as an object of art ("This line should be just a little longer... this side looks too heavy. ..."). Wilson likens the image of the bed to "a death box... a coffin."

As we prepare to work on III–3 (III–4 in Büchner; Auletta has cut the III–3 prison scene and combined it with later scenes), the scene in which Danton is first brought before the Tribunal, we discuss whether or not the National Convention and the Tribunal can be the same space. Though they serve separate functions, one legislative, the other judicial, they are both spaces of power, judgment and speech. We decide that making them one place will actually confuse the audience less than if we tried to distinguish between them. This allows Herman, who presides over the

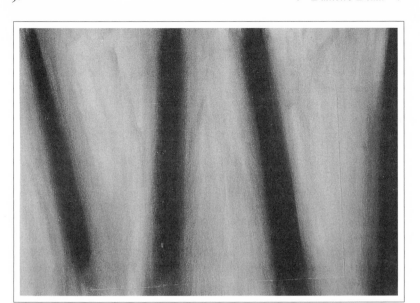

Charcoal drawing by Robert Wilson, 1992, titled Danton's Death, *Act III, Scene 6. Photograph by Art Industrial.*

Tribunal, to preside also over the Convention, as the forbidding image of corrupt authority and tainted justice.

We look at pictures of the historic Tribunal and Convention for ideas of spatial relationships and staging. Wilson remembers a chair he designed for another production that he would like to use again for St. Just and Robespierre in the Convention. He also redesigns the president's chair as a more imposing sculpture: a severe black lacquer chair with a tall, thin back that is mirrored by a long tongue extending several feet from the base. A flaming torch stands beside it. John Conklin creates a mock-up with blocks of wood and black fabric until a more sturdy version can be built.

Later, in rehearsals, we are reminded that occasionally the method of using chance to match text and movement, intended to rescue the gestures from illustration of the words, produces completely opposite results. While placing the numbered moves of the first Tribunal scene with the text, Richard delivers the line "I stand before you now," just as Wilson calls out the number that requires Richard to step directly in front of Herman. "STOP!" Wilson shouts. "Stop. I can't believe it. You try and you try to keep it from looking stupid, and it doesn't matter."

June 20–22

Wilson in Germany for technical rehearsals of *Black Rider*. Ann-Christin and the company take the opportunity to catch up and review the week's blocking.

June 23

Wilson is now convinced that his original idea for the execution will have to be reconsidered. The column of very cold, white light against a background of white is changed in favor of some object that actually represents the guillotine. He looks at drawings and paintings of guillotines. Inspired by a drawing of the public beheading of Johann Christian Woyzeck, Wilson sketches a simple, large, wooden box: the guillotine. The men will walk to the top on hidden stairs and, as they are executed, sink into the box. The guillotine blade has become pure movement: somehow a sharp-edged field of white will cut across the black of the stage floor.

June 24: Morning

The floor of the rehearsal hall is covered with a thin film of charcoal dust that clings to the actor's feet and clothes. It is the byproduct of Wilson's late-night work in the hall making charcoal drawings of each scene in *Danton's Death*. The drawings hang around the hall and almost completely cover the back wall. It gives the effect of some crude private gallery, or of scenery: a black-and-white charcoal-sketched backdrop of frenzied lines and mysterious shapes. Whereas the storyboard sketches are working plans from which to create the physical production, these are works of art, drawings not bound to any function of illustrating or explaining the text. They will, most likely, end up in galleries and collections. With these drawings, Wilson develops a visual language of the piece—light, space, line—that allows a freer, more abstract exploration of the play.

June 25–26

Wilson begins to concern himself more with "edges"—highlighting juxtapositions and contradictions within the piece. As we review, Richard, especially, continues to try new variations and gestures. These changes are sometimes inspired by the text, but are often just experimentation with movement. The actors also begin to focus more on the cold, hard line delivery.

June 27

During a lunch break, John Conklin shows Wilson preliminary costume sketches. Most of the sketches are very simple, with little color—blacks, grays and browns. The costumes of Julie and Robespierre are green and red, respectively. The drawings suggest clothing of the late eighteenth to early nineteenth century, somewhere between the time of the French Revolution and Büchner's writing of the play.

In the afternoon we have our first run-through of the entire piece. We are all amazed and relieved at how well it has come together, and the actors feel proud of the accomplishment. The work to be done is obvious. The actors, having spent little time exploring the text, look forward to an opportunity to do so in Phase C. Some sections of the script are unclear and will have to be changed. Most importantly, the run-through gives us the first good experience of the play's rhythm and how pacing, musical bridges and scene transitions are all integral to the structure. The piece moves towards certain scenes (Danton in the field; Robespierre alone; Julie's death), rests there, suspended in time, and then rushes toward the next resting point. To build to these scenes, the play must move quickly, with few pauses. "We have to earn the weight," says Wilson. He wants to keep the production from being oppressive: "I don't want this to be a depressing play, this play called *Danton's Death.*" While giving notes, he indicates what the actors should begin to do on their own:

> I separate the text and blocking to create tension, but it should never seem arbitrary. Eventually, the elements are not separate, they form a complete whole. In a formal theatre, the actors *do* have characters and ideas and emotions, but they have to structure it for themselves and they can't force an audience to accept this structure. I like the actors to find those ideas on their own, without the director interfering too much, as long as what the actor is doing doesn't interfere with the broader ideas and structure; and as long as the actor is not imposing a particular idea on the audience.
>
> I resist creating subtext, but I like it when actors build a subtext that I can't decipher, when I don't know exactly what is going on. The form is always boring. One has to fill the form with many colors, attitudes, and ideas. It's what you do inside of the form that is interesting. One must take the frame and make it one's own.

We have another run-through that is videotaped so there will be a reference for the actors in September. In his notes, Wilson urges everyone not to think of the slow, stylized movement as being in slow motion. It is not an intellectual concept, Wilson insists, but rather something one experiences. He also reiterates the internal work that the actors will have to do:

> A good actor has to be blind and deaf as well as hearing and seeing. Being blind, one has an interior reflection that becomes noble. One of the big differences between naturalism and formalism is that in formalism it is all noble. Even if you are playing a whore or a beggar, it is all noble.

June 28: Sunday

The *Bauprobe*. The set for the Alley's summer production has been removed from the Large Stage for one day. In the wings are mock-ups of scenery, properties, and furniture pieces. Wood, cardboard, Styrofoam and paper serve as the primary materials of a rudimentary set.

Stephen Strawbridge has provided a very basic lighting plot, and John Conklin is working with Technical Director Tony Bish to make sure that every set and furniture piece has some kind of model that approximates the size and shape of its final form.

When the acting company arrives, they begin patiently walking through their blocking for each scene. Though very little focus is on the actors, it is an opportunity for them to explore the actual playing space and point out potential problems and new opportunities.

The *Bauprobe* becomes a major event at the theatre. A photographer chronicles the work. Anne Bogart and Tadashi Suzuki,

Richard Thomas and Robert Wilson during Phase B workshop. Photograph by Jim Caldwell.

in town for meetings, watch some of the proceedings. Though it is Sunday, and the day's performance has been canceled, there is a steady flow of staff members sneaking in to witness the rehearsal. It is our first glimpse of the April sketches realized on the stage.

Gradually, the technical and logistical problems of the design and staging are tackled. We discover that the positions of the downstage legs, which create a kind of false proscenium, interfere too much with sight lines, and so must be moved. Wilson makes decisions on the shape and dimensions of the marble sofa and the bathtub. The pool is redesigned. The actors are repositioned to account for new dimensions of the prison. Chairs are designed for Robespierre and St. Just for the end of Act II.

Time runs out before we reach the end of the play, but we have gone far enough for the actors to have a fairly accurate impression of what the physical production will be like. The *Bauprobe*, and Phase B, is over.

July–September 1992

The scene shop builds the deck and shutters and constructs new rehearsal mock-ups. Sculptor Ben Woitena, who will make the marble sofa, begins to turn four thousand pounds of marble into Wilson's design. After the production, the Alley will be able to sell the sofa at auction; Wilson has donated it to the Alley. Bob Auletta rewrites scenes II-2 and III-7 as song lyrics and a revised script is disseminated mid-July.

PHASE C: REHEARSALS
AND TECHNICAL REHEARSALS

September 22: Tuesday

It does not seem as if three months have passed since the *Bauprobe* as we reconvene in the rehearsal hall. Wilson, in Spain, will not arrive until September 30. Ann-Christin begins the rehearsals with a simple introduction: "We were hoping you would do thinking, not homework. We'll spend the next few days trying to get back to where we left off." We will also use the time to incorporate discoveries and alterations made in the *Bauprobe*.

Since most of the cast is currently performing in the Alley's production of *The Front Page*, rehearsals are limited to the daytime until October 12. Wilson's absence, instead of being a hindrance, is actually helpful in taking the pressure off the actors during this difficult period of reconstruction.

Newly joining the cast are Tommy Derrah as the Tribunal's prosecutor, Fouquier; and Peter Webster as its president, Herman. Scott Rabinowitz will play Camille, formerly played by Willis Sparks, who will move into the role of Legendre.

The cast reads the revised script. Deborah Kinghorn again

goes over pronunciations, and I review the historical and literary background of the play and characters. Some of the actors have used the interim to read about the Revolution and to do research on their characters, but at least one confides to me that his research was of little help. He spent the interim concentrating on finding a meaning for each of his gestures.

To refresh everyone's memory, we watch the videotape of the June 27 run-through. This first chance for the company to see the piece in its entirety jogs the memory and gives a good overview of the play's structure.

September 23–27

The time away has allowed new ideas to surface and the actors feel some freedom to try new things—a new line, a different gesture, altered timing, a new point of view. Ann-Christin encourages this experimentation: "Find a meaning for each gesture. If you have a movement that absolutely makes no sense to you, don't do it, change it. Find the meaning for yourself."

In the interim Richard has compared Auletta's adaptation to a translation of the full text, and has many ideas for changes, mostly additions, that we try out during the week. Ann-Christin and the actors adjust their choreography to accommodate changes and I communicate with Bob Auletta by phone, often taking dictation of rewritten lines and speeches.

The actors are beginning to "fill the form," working inwardly to construct their characters and make connections between words and movement. The week becomes much more than review, it becomes a period of rediscovery.

The new cast members have the more difficult task, and much of this week is spent with them. Since all of their choreography was generated by other actors, they first have to learn it and

Marissa Chibas (Julie) and Richard Thomas on stage with mock-up of Danton's bed during the Bauprobe. *Photograph by Jim Caldwell.*

then make it their own. Tommy and Peter develop interesting physical characteristics: Fouquier acquires an eerie rictus, and Herman, a quirky, falconlike posture. We attempt to further clarify their characters—important, because in this adaptation they are the only representatives of the Tribunal—and a speech previously assigned to Herman is given to Fouquier.

The cast learns the music and lyrics for street scenes II-2 and III-7, but since the songs are much different than the spoken text, the scene will have to be reworked once Wilson returns. For now, the actors do the best they can incorporating the songs with the old framework.

This week is also a productive one for Joe Pino and the sound department, as they record any text that will be part of the final sound design, allowing Joe to have tapes in rehearsal when Wilson returns.

September 30

Wilson arrives from Spain, and we have a run-through for him. Some of the scenes have taken on new qualities. The first scene, for instance, has become very fast and its humor takes us by surprise. Afterwards, Wilson thanks the company for their hard work and begins to give notes. He stops. "If I pause a lot," he says, "it's because I'm used to having someone translate everything I say."

Because there are so many scenes, it is important that we work toward keeping the piece moving by making the transitions very quick and by using sound and music as bridges. Wilson tells the actors to place the tensions in their performances intelligently, and not always be at one hundred percent. "One can always hold back, leave a little space. That's space for the audience."

It is agreed that we will run one or two acts at each rehearsal from now on. Whereas the scene became the basic working unit in Phase B, this process will focus on the structure and pacing of acts and the entire piece, as well as on individual moments. This latter work Wilson calls "detailing."

October 1

Wilson and Scott Rabinowitz discuss I-1. Though Scott has learned Camille's moves, they do not seem to make sense either in terms of Camille's character or of the scene as a whole. We are also challenged by his first, long speech, filled with similes and mythological imagery. How should this be delivered? Camille is proving to be the most problematic character in the production. The poetic, passionate, sentimental Camille seems at odds with Wilson's formal, unsentimental production. Perhaps, of these eighteenth-century characters, he is the most eighteenth century of them all.

Taking his cue from Camille's political rhetoric ("Let the constitution be a transparent veil, clinging close to the body of the people. . . . We want our gods and goddesses to be naked and to be free and easy with themselves."), Wilson reblocks the speech so Camille is more involved with the prone bodies of Herault and the card-playing prostitutes.

Scene I-3. The scene is Robespierre's address to the Jacobins, in which he justifies the Terror and incites his colleagues to commit further violence. Büchner also has him deliver a short history of the Terror, or "who we've killed and why." Wilson asks Lou to do the speech very quickly, one long arc to the end, with only one or two pauses. The speech is very long, even in Auletta's abridged version, and it is difficult to sustain the energetic delivery Wilson is asking for. If Lou performs the speech in this way, we may need to make further cuts.

October 2

The first image, what the audience sees as they enter the theatre, has been decided. Onstage will be the president's chair, the lighted torch and a book. Wilson reminds us all that the two most important moments of a production are the first and the last, and so he takes his time to create the looks and sounds that will precede the first line of the play. Chuck has composed a hymnlike organ score for the opening, to which Joe gradually adds sound of glass and wood breaking, ending in a deafening roar. Wilson likes the loud, overpowering sound leading to the debauchery and fast-paced feeling of the brothel. "Usually," says Wilson, "I start my pieces very quietly. This one starts very chaotic and then settles. Usually my pieces don't have any rhythm until the end. This one is different."

A new character is added to the opening sequence as well as to the Tribunal and Convention scenes. This silent figure, dubbed "The Keeper of the Flame," will light and extinguish the torch, and be responsible for striking it in transitions.

After a run of Acts I and II, Wilson examines the mock-up for the Tribunal chairs. Though he likes its proportions, he tries to find an interesting way for Robespierre to sit in it. "What if these arms could pivot," Wilson asks, breaking the arms in demonstration. The chairs, using the broken mock-up as a model, will, indeed, be made with pivoting arms.

October 3

Scene IV-5 (Büchner's IV-6). Julie's suicide. Marissa lies on what will be a low, thin black bed that rests on four small pyramids. A long, black cylinder serves as a headrest; beside her, a small vial. We hear the ocean and children playing. She speaks softly into a body microphone. It is a beautiful, simple text:

> Earth's features have changed now, her face so calm, beautiful, grave as a dying woman's. She drifts like a corpse down the river of space. Is there no arm to pull her from the water, to kiss her and bury her? I must not keep him waiting, even for a moment.

Wilson asks her to put space around the words "beautiful" and "grave," to break the words free of their syntactical meanings. He urges her not to be sentimental. Despite this, the scene resonates with a profound sadness.

October 6

Run-through. The room is filled with new charcoal drawings. Now, whenever Act I is run, so too is the preshow sequence, including sound and the lighting cues approximated with the overhead lights. Tree, with stopwatch, calls out what the stage looks like at the appropriate time intervals. Wilson insists that this sequence be perfectly coordinated. "Latecomers can be seated in scene two," he says. "People who come after that will have to stand in the back."

October 7

Act III. The transitions in this act take too long and are making for a slow beginning to the second half. For III-2, Wilson has designed an 8′ x 8′ x 8′ gauze box, in which Fouquier and Herman conspire to fix Danton's jury. The transition to it from the scenically complicated prison in III-1 is deadly in length. We search for a solution. Bettye Fitzpatrick as the Jailor stands outside of the prison downstage at the end of III-1, and Wilson suggests that she could do or say something to cover the shift. While looking for an appropriate passage from material that has been cut, I remember the bizarre story the grandmother tells the children in *Woyzeck*. It begins:

> Once upon a time there was a little girl who had no
> father and no mother. Everyone was dead. There was
> no one left in the whole, wide world. So she went to
> the moon and it was a piece of rotten wood . . .

It is a cynical fairy tale of alienation and despair. Though I am intrigued by this speech, especially in the gravelly, folksy way I

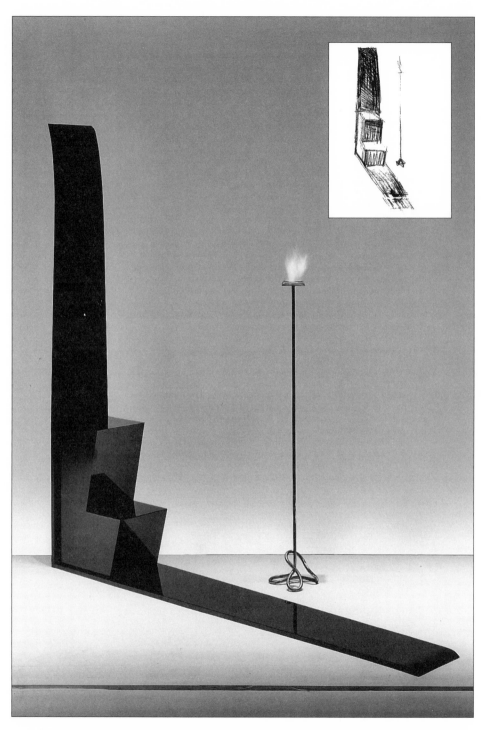

Wilson's sketch and final version of The President's Chair. *Photograph by Paul Hester.*

am sure Bettye will deliver it, I am not sure if it will work, or if it will seem out of place or odd. But then, it is odd in *Woyzeck* too. Ann-Christin likes it and we give it to Bettye, who reads it aloud. Wilson decides to try it for a while.

October 12

Final run-through of play with Wilson before technical rehearsals start. Tomorrow he is in Tokyo to oversee lighting rehearsals for *Einstein on the Beach*.

There are still problems with the rhythm of the piece, and some of the transitions continue to stop the play's momentum. I am particularly worried that there are long stretches in which it is simply too difficult to follow the logic of the play. Though elucidation of plot is not one of the primary intents of this production, we also do not want the audience to confuse one character with another, or to miss important information.

In the evening, the actors walk quickly through the blocking so that Wilson can discuss with Stephen Strawbridge an outline of the lighting for each scene: intensity of light, whose faces should be lit with spots, how tightly shuttered a special should be, the highlights on a hand or foot and what color gel a particular spot must have. The spots must be strong, he says, because isolating the faces is so important. We will need plenty of 201 gel, which corrects the amber light of an incandescent source and gives Wilson the cool, white light he desires. He goes very quickly, moving around in the space with the actors. The structuring of light, which will take so much of our attention next week, begins to take shape. "I never see a piece until after it's lit," says Wilson. "The lighting is a wholly different structure."

October 13–18

Wilson in Tokyo. We use this time to review and clarify each scene, trying to solve any problems of staging before the technical rehearsals begin and the focus shifts away from the actors. It is a last opportunity to do intensive vocal and textual work, and we continue to refine the speeches of Robespierre and St. Just at the end of Act II.

This time is also used to work on the production book that we will publish. This book will be supplementary to the playbill, and will include the visual book, some of Wilson's drawings, photographs from all stages of the process, information about Büchner and the play, and short essays by Gregory Boyd and Wilson.

October 19: Monday

Wilson returns in the evening and lighting rehearsals begin. As it is the Equity day off, Wilson works with "The Keeper of the Flame," Matt Rippy, on the opening sequence. Rippy is given a series of crosses and gestures that will take half an hour to perform.

In Phase B, Wilson started with a structure of time and the visual book and then proceeded intuitively within those frameworks. In these rehearsals, he similarly relies on structures—the choreography and text as well as the visual book—to allow him the freedom to experiment and improvise in the creation of the lighting. Playing with the smallest, almost imperceptible changes in color and intensity, Wilson creates a series of looks for the opening. He works like a painter, using light as his medium. The cyclorama changes from blue to white to red. The book, the torch and the president's chair are isolated in cold, tightly shuttered light. A lone figure walks enigmatically through this austere landscape.

Act I, Scene 1. John Feltch (Herault) with the prostitutes. Photograph by Jim Caldwell.

October 20–21

We move slowly, lighting four to five scenes in a ten-hour day. A single cue can take thirty minutes to build. Often Wilson creates a series of looks for the cyclorama that are numbered and cued into the scene later, in the same way he matched movements to text in Phase B. In addition to lighting, we also focus on the correct positions and movement of the panels.

Meanwhile, the actors learn their makeup designs from Designer Debra Coleman. The faces are very white with extreme definition on the cheekbones and nose. Depending on the lighting, the women do achieve the light porcelain look Wilson admired in the David portraits. The men tend to look more ghostly, cadaverlike.

October 22

The theatre is very quiet. A pair of observers laugh at some joke between themselves. Wilson gives them an angry lecture. "This is not television," he admonishes them. The atmosphere is respectful, with all attention directed toward the work onstage.

The pace of the work will have to pick up if we plan to keep on schedule. The very real prospect of not having a run-through before the first preview begins to worry the actors and running crew. The actors have no way of knowing how the play will come across, how the audience will respond. Their experience up to now has been the rarefied atmosphere of the rehearsal hall, or the plodding of technical rehearsals. Though this is the case for any production, the jump from rehearsal hall to performance seems to be a greater one for this project. This is paradoxical, because the highly structured nature of this process will perforce make the performances much more like the rehearsal run-throughs than in a more conventional production.

October 23–27

We have fallen behind schedule by a day. At this rate, we will have no technical rehearsals with sound and the first full run-through will be in front of an audience on first preview. Wilson, however, does not seem overly concerned.

Joe, Chuck and the sound crew are on a different schedule than the rest of the company. From noon until 9:00 p.m., they record, mix and edit the music and sound cues. They then move into the theatre to set levels and to cue the show until 4:00 or 5:00 a.m. Since the actors are gone, Joe uses the videotape of the June 27 run-through to tech the production.

Finally, we get to the last three scenes. These are the most difficult to tech, in part because we did not get to them in the *Bauprobe*.

Downstage, we see Danton, his associates, the carter and prostitutes. They walk en masse, a traveling tableau making a back and forth path to the guillotine. Upstage, the cyclorama is very white. Slowly, the wooden box moves from left to right across the back of the stage. As the group makes their upstage cross, a white drop, hidden in a lip of the stage, is pulled out to cover the deck in a field of white. A hard, white edge moves across the black stage. A blade. The prostitutes exit, leaving the condemned, the carter (James Black) and the executioner (Bettye Fitzpatrick). The men one by one ascend the hidden stairs to the top of the box. There they each step on a trap door and slowly disappear. The last two to be executed are Herault and Danton. They try to embrace, but the executioner stops them. Danton asks:

> Do you really think you can be crueler than death? Do
> you really think you can prevent our heads from kiss-
> ing, there in the basket?

First Herault descends, then Danton. Our attention is drawn to the ramp on the far left side of the house, where Lucille, now mad, contemplates her husband's execution.

> Oh Camille. Where shall I look for you now?

She exits. Onstage, James and Bettye have climbed atop the box and deliver a drunken song. James performs a fly *lazzi*. They start to leave as we see Lucille making her way towards the stage through the audience. She steps onto the now-white stage and approaches the box.

> Oh angel of death, may I sit in your lap?

From behind the box we hear James and Bettye shout, "Who's there?" They enter from either side, staring down at Lucille, who utters the defiant, suicidal lines "Long live the King." The lights go out.

October 27: Wednesday

Before first preview. Wilson talks to the actors about this new step in the process:

> Now is the time that the piece grows, becomes yours. It's no longer mine. It's difficult to talk about emotion. I often fail as a director to produce deep emotion— not cheap sentiment, but something that is authentic. That, right now, is lacking. This is something I don't know how to tell you to produce or feel. Sometimes it is a state of mind. I don't want you to push too much or to think too much, but to find something that is deep, personal. . . .
>
> The whole piece can be lighter. Don't anticipate: "I know I have to go over there but I don't know how I'm going to get there." So when you do, it is a surprise. Listen to the audience all the time. Be ahead of them. Get your headline first. Tell a very simple story. Then you can fill it with a million things, but start simply. There are still parts that are stiff and times when you need to fill the room. Don't push, but you have to know that even a small simple gesture can fill a room.

The moment before Danton sinks into the box is not right. The other characters speak just before they descend, but Danton has no line and must wait for Herault to go down first. I suggest we try an idea that kept coming up in rehearsals: Danton speaking his historical parting line, "Show my head to the people. It will be well worth the effort." Büchner must have known about this apocryphal attribution and chose not to include it, but it helps us to isolate Danton's moment of death and so we will try it. Tonight we will also try Bettye and James not coming out to arrest Lucille at the end. We will still hear the shouts, but the last image will be only of Lucille.

Evening. First preview (and first full technical run-through). The actors, somewhat tired, but ready for an audience, do well. The performance is workmanlike, and one can imagine them counting out their movements beneath their breath. With a few minor exceptions the technical aspects run smoothly. Most of the problems are, as expected, with the sound.

What is striking is that the visual structure, now fully realized, has changed little from those initial drawings Wilson created in February.

October 28–30

Rehearsals and previews. The sound and music get the most attention in the next few days. Levels and cues are changed in an attempt to connect the twenty-eight scenes sonically as much as possible. In performance, the actors are trusting the form now, discovering more moments of truthful expression. Richard is especially sensitive to the audience, and his speeches before the Tribunal become more and more powerful as he explores the highs and lows of each speech.

The audiences for the second, third and fourth previews are large and follow the production well. About fifty people leave at intermission each night, but by Friday I already recognize people who are seeing the show a second time. By Thursday morning, most of Wilson's notes are about pacing. He also encourages the cast to keep working internally:

> It's a little forced right now, a little forced to the audience. It's all right to do that; it's theatre, it's a show. But I miss the personal moments, the times you are performing for yourself. Something that touches us. It's how you feel about what you do that makes it special. It's not something manufactured, but something real . . .
>
> Find the moments of interior reflection. . . . So often theatre doesn't have that interior reflection. It's difficult. The audience is conditioned by television, so it's a struggle. So often what we experience is framed by the television screen and so our audio and visual perception is framed. We are trying to break the frame, so the audio and visual experience is boundless. That's why I hate interpretation, it limits the audience's opportunity, their mental space for reflection.

Richard asks if there are specific places where Wilson feels the production is too interpretive. "Yes," answers Wilson, "but I won't tell you because then you'll try to act it. Just keep asking yourself, checking yourself. . . . Just keep working. It takes time . . ."

October 31–November 15

Performances. The actors continue to find those places of reflection that Wilson talked about and to fill their choreography with their personal "meanings." The production is, in a few scenes, transcendental, evoking emotions without being emotional—Marion's angelic cross behind Danton in the field; Julie giving a young boy a lock of her hair to tell Danton she will join him in death; Lucille's seductive madness; Danton's final night in prison.

Before each performance, on the Alley's Arena Stage, I give a brief, half-hour talk about the play, Wilson's work and what to look for in the production. Though the Alley presents at least one preshow discussion for each of our productions, this is the first time we have held one before every performance. We have done as much as possible to prepare our audience through our newsletter and program, and these talks help people be less afraid of an *avant-garde* production, without telling them what to think. They are well attended and many come up to me after the production to ask questions or to discuss the play.

As many times as I have seen the production, I am still astonished by the final thirty minutes—when, briefly, these characters, these Revolutionary ciphers, seem to transform into spiritual creatures. The last image—Lucille sits by the side of the box (inexplicably, it seems; there is no chair), her head moving ever so slightly to one side, as if presenting her neck to the guillotine blade, isolated in the cold, cold light—gives me the feeling of being in the presence of ghosts.

A German critic said he admired this production because it treated one of the most political of all plays apolitically. I disagree. By rejecting emotionalism and melodrama, the production lets us listen to political oratory in a way in which we are unaccustomed: evaluating substance over style and ideas over personality. By stripping away historical trappings, presenting instead a series of solitary speakers, Wilson asks us to ponder the power—and danger—of the act of speech itself.

Finally, we witness the silencing of one whose greatest gift is that of speech, whose greatest contribution is in the realm of ideas. In Act III, Herman rings a bell, the official call for order, trying to stop Danton's speech to the Tribunal. But Danton, fighting with his only weapon, cries out:

Bettye Fitzpatrick (Executioner), Richard Thomas and James Black (Carter) in Act IV, Scene 7. Photograph by Jim Caldwell.

The sound of a man defending his life will always be louder than your little bell.

On November 3, after giving my pre-performance talk, in which I discuss Jacobins and moderates, political rhetoric and the forces of history, I go home to watch the 1992 election returns.

There is a peculiar discrepancy between the Hollywood packaging and sound-bite attention span of the current political campaigns and the battleground of ideas in Büchner's fictional

Revolution. Given the absence of substantive discourse, and the obfuscating bombast surrounding issues of artistic expression and freedom of speech (especially at one political party's nominating convention held here in Houston), one can not help appreciating the idealistic debates Büchner fashions for us, nor the careful way Wilson sets them as rare and precious stones to be examined and admired.

⇥⇤⇥⇤⇥⇥⇤⇥⇤⇥⇤⇥⇤⇥⇤⇥⇤⇥⇤⇥⇤⇥⇤⇥⇤⇥⇤⇥⇤⇥⇤⇥⇤⇥⇤⇥⇤
Special thanks to the Byrd Hoffman Foundation,
Gregory Boyd, Nina Chwast and, of course, Robert Wilson.
⇥⇤⇥⇤⇥⇤⇥⇤⇥⇥⇤⇥⇤⇥⇤⇥⇤⇥⇤⇥⇤⇥⇤⇥⇤⇥⇤⇥⇤⇥⇤⇥⇤⇥⇤⇥⇤⇥⇤

Christopher Baker served as Resident Dramaturg at the Alley Theatre in Houston and at the Shakespeare Theatre in Washington, D.C. He has worked with directors such as Anne Bogart, Adrian Hall, Andrei Serban and Robert Wilson. He is a dramaturg and director at PlayMakers Repertory Company in Chapel Hill, NC, and a visiting assistant professor at the University of North Carolina at Chapel Hill.

SELECT BIBLIOGRAPHY

Ausstellungshallen Mathildenhöhe Darmstadt et al. *Georg Büchner: Revolutionär, Dicter, Wissenschaftler 1813–1837: Ausstellung, Mathild-enhöhe, Darmstadt, 2. August bis 27. September 1987: der Katalog.* Basel: Stroemfeld/Roter-Stern, 1987.

Büchner, Georg. *Complete Works and Letters.* Translated by Henry J. Schmidt. Edited by Walter Hinderer and Henry J. Schmidt. New York: Continuum, 1986.

———. *Danton's Death: A New Version.* [Adapted] by Howard Brenton from a translation by Jane Fry. London: Methuen, 1982.

———. *Danton's Tod and Woyzeck.* Edited by Margaret Jacobs. Manchester, England: Manchester University Press, 1963.

———. *Gesammelte Werke.* Edited by Kasimir Edschmid. Vienna: K. Desch, 1963.

———. *Plays of Georg Büchner.* Translated by Geoffrey Dunlop. New York: I. Ravin, 1952.

Chapman, Pauline. *The French Revolution: As Seen by Madame Tussaud, Witness Extraordinary.* London: Quiller Press, 1989.

Danton. Motion picture based on Stanislawa Przybyszewska's play, *L'Affaire Danton.* Director: Andrzej Wajda. 1982.

Dowd, David Lloyd. *Pageant-master of the Republic: Jacques-Louis David and the French Revolution.* Lincoln: University of Nebraska Press, 1948.

Friedlaender, Walter. *David to Delacroix.* Translated by Robert Gold-water. New York: Schocken Books, 1968.

Grab, Walter. *The French Revolution, the Beginning of Modern Democracy.* Translated by Terry Bond. London: Bracken Books, 1989.

Grimm, Reinhold. *Love, Lust and Rebellion: New Approaches to Georg Büchner.* Madison: University of Wisconsin Press, 1985.

Hampson, Norman. *The Life and Opinions of Maximilien Robespierre.* London: Duckworth, 1974.

Hibbert, Christopher. *The Days of the French Revolution.* New York: Morrow, 1980.

Hilton, Julian. *Georg Büchner.* New York: Grove Press, 1982.

Johann, Ernst. *Georg Büchner in Selbstzeugnissen und Bilddokumenten.* Hamburg: Rowohlt, 1958.

Loomis, Stanley. *Paris in the Terror.* Philadelphia: Lippincott, 1964.

Maurois, Andre. *J.-L. David.* Paris: Editions du Dimanche, 1948.

Mueller, Carl Richard, translator. Introduction to *Georg Büchner, Complete Plays and Prose.* New York: Hill and Wang, 1963.

Nanteuil, Luc de. *Jacques-Louis David.* New York: Abrams, 1985.

Palmer, R. R. *Twelve Who Ruled.* Princeton: Princeton University Press, 1970.

Richards, David Gleyre. *Georg Büchner and the Birth of the Modern Drama.* Albany: State University of New York Press, 1977.

Schama, Simon. *Citizens.* New York: Knopf, 1989.

Schmidt, Henry J. *Satire, Caricature and Perspectivism in the Works of Georg Büchner.* Stanford Studies in Germanics and Slavics, no. 8. The Hague: Mouton, 1970.

Schnapper, Antoine, et al., editors. *Jacques-Louis David.* Paris: Eds. de le Réunion des musées nationaux, 1989.

Sérullaz, Maurice. *Eugène Delacroix.* New York: H. N. Abrams, 1971.

Soboul, Albert. *A Short History of the French Revolution, 1789–1799.* Translated by Geoffrey Symcox. Berkeley: University of California Press, 1977.

Viehweg, Wolfram. *Georg Büchners "Dantons Tod" auf dem deutschen Theater.* München: Laokoon-Verlag, 1964.

Whitham, J. Mills. *A Biographical History of the French Revolution.* Freeport, NY: Books for Libraries Press, 1968.

The $\mathcal{L}$OVE SPACE DEMANDS

AT CROSSROADS THEATRE COMPANY

by Shelby Jiggetts

Ntozake Shange, author of *for colored girls who've considered suicide/ when the rainbow is enuf* and, more recently, *Betsey Brown*, collaborated with the Crossroads Theatre Company from 1990–92 to develop a new performance work based on her book of poetry, *The Love Space Demands: A Continuing Saga*. The resulting multimedia work on the African-American experience and on the topics of sex and love called upon Shange's celebrated gifts as poet/dancer/ performer. *The Love Space Demands*, directed by Talvin Wilks, was performed at the Crossroads Theatre Company in New Brunswick, New Jersey, in the spring of 1992. Shelby Jiggetts was literary manager of Crossroads and dramaturg for this production.

BY	Ntozake Shange
DIRECTOR	Talvin Wilks
COMPOSER/MUSIC DIRECTOR	William "Spaceman" Patterson
CHOREOGRAPHER	Mickey Davidson
PHOTOGRAPHIC ENVIRONMENTAL DESIGNER	Adál
MULTIMEDIA SET DESIGN COORDINATOR	Anton C. Nelessen
SET DESIGNER	Richard Carroll
COSTUME DESIGNER	Toni-Leslie James
LIGHTING DESIGNER	Heather Carson
SOUND DESIGNER	Carmen Whiip
DRAMATURG	Shelby Jiggetts
PRODUCTION STAGE MANAGER	Patreshettarlini Adams

THE ENSEMBLE

Demitri Corbin
Ezra Knight
Billy Patterson
Jackie Mari Roberts
Ntozake Shange
Theara J. Ward

THE MUSICIANS

Guitar, Keyboards, Guitar Synthesizer, Pocket Trumpet, Background Vocals	Billy "Spaceman" Patterson
Keyboards, Background Vocals	Dinky Bingham
Drums, Synth Drums	Dengal Warren Benbow

INTRODUCTION

Writing this now, I don't for the life of me remember why I (and not Sydné Mahone, Crossroads Theatre's director of play development) was assigned the gig as dramaturg of Ntozake Shange's *The Love Space Demands*. I was very young in my career. I was in my second season with the company in the summer of 1990 when Mahone first broached the subject of working with Shange to adapt the volume of poems to the stage.

The journey began in 1990 and continued until February 1992. Taking the trip were a great American writer, a young director making his professional debut and a cadre of gifted collaborators.

At the time I felt useless. At the time I wondered why I was in this profession. At the time I wished I'd gone to grad school—for physics. At the time I felt immense pride in our director, Talvin Wilks; healthy respect for Ntozake Shange (author of *for colored girls who've considered suicide/when the rainbow is enuf* and *Betsey Brown*); and a sense of wonder for Crossroads Theatre Company and our wonderfully committed staff and audience. At the time I wished that I didn't need the commission money for this notebook to finance a move to New York, so that I could hide the journal in a drawer and never face my ineffectiveness again. Each attempt to create something new brings out the best in us always and the worst in us sometimes. I now realize that the most we can ever do is never to make the same mistake twice and to hope that the work will outlast us all.

→←

Ntozake Shange's *The Love Space Demands*, like much of her previous work, enjoyed a life as a published volume of poetry and
as a performance piece. When Sydné Mahone first discussed the
possibility of developing the work with Shange, the volume had
not yet been published and Shange, along with musician/composer
William "Spaceman" Patterson, had been performing excerpts from
the collection for years at a variety of venues that included the
Painted Bride in Philadelphia, where Shange lives.

Our first step was to shape the excerpts into an evening
and to establish a relationship between Shange and the man chosen to direct the work-in-progress—Talvin Wilks. In the tradition
of the Crossroads "artistrator," Wilks was working as the theatre's
development coordinator as well as an unofficial artist-in-
residence. In 1989, Crossroads world-premiered Wilks' play *Tod,
the Boy, Tod*. In the coming seasons we had hoped to offer him
opportunities to direct, and the Shange project seemed a perfect
gig.

The Love Space Demands began life at Crossroads as part
of Genesis, our new works festival, in March 1991. When the multimedia piece, presented as a work-in-progress, was well received
by the Crossroads' audience, Artistic Director Ricardo Khan
made the commitment to a full production for the spring of our
1991–92 season. Khan also decided that in order to realize its fullest
potential, the production should include an ensemble of performers
in addition to Shange and Patterson. With that decision, Shange
agreed to perform as part of an ensemble for the first time in twenty
years.

The further development of the piece included a one-week
workshop with actors in the fall of 1991. Wilks also used a series
of scheduled residencies at historically black colleges as an oppor-

Author Ntozake Shange. Slide projection photograph by Adál.

tunity to explore the text. In February 1992, Crossroads Theatre
world-premiered *The Love Space Demands*.

Prior to the full production there were changes in concept
and context; two sets of actors; blessedly more harmony than
disharmony, but enough of the latter to make you go "Hmmm"; a
young company attempting to meet the challenge; and a veteran
artist still willing to challenge herself after twenty years.

The epiphany of orgasms or infatuations is a consistently sought after reward for leading an otherwise rea-
sonable life. But the transmissions of sexual disease,
including AIDS, now associated with such coming
together weigh heavily on choices baby-boomers had
come to make with leisure . . .

Our behaviors were just beginning to change
when the epidemic began, moving sex closer to shame
now than anytime since I've been alive. Words and attitudes that undermine trust and liberty to feel are
creeping back into the bedrooms and couches of our
lives, so that we are always second-guessing each other.
When that fails, the artificial highs of cocaine, crack,
methamphetamine, heroin, alcohol, compulsive sex or
compulsive suffering come sauntering down the street
and into our vacant, yearning lives. The sanctity of an
inner quiet and clarity present in the spirit is the least
that opening up to another person requires. When we
don't know what we mean or why we are doing what
we do, we are only able to bring chaos and pain to ourselves and others.

I didn't know what was being said to me, sometimes. Sometimes, I couldn't fathom why any of us
were doing what we were doing and calling ourselves

somebody's beloved. The poems and monologues in *The Love Space Demands* and *I Heard Eric Dolphy in His Eyes* are real questions I have asked and the sharp edges of the answers.

—Ntozake Shange

From the Introduction to

The Love Space Demands: A Continuing Saga, 1992

Summer 1990

Sydné Mahone (director of play development at Crossroads Theatre) informs the company that Ntozake Shange is interested in working with Crossroads on the development of a new performance piece based on her upcoming volume of poetry entitled *The Love Space Demands: A Continuing Saga*. Everyone's hope is that Shange will perform in March as part of our new works festival, Genesis 1991: A Festival of New Voices at Crossroads Theatre. Shange provides us with a copy of the uncorrected proof of the unpublished manuscript.

The titles of the poems included in the manuscript are:

"irrepressibly bronze, beautiful & mine"
"even tho yr sampler broke down on you"
"serial monogamy"
"intermittent celibacy"
"a third generation geechee myth for yr birthday"
"loosening strings or give me an 'A' "
"m.e.s.l. (male english as a second language): in defense of
    bilingualism"
"devotion from one lover to another"
"if i go all the way without you where would i go?"
"i heard eric dolphy in his eyes"
"crack annie"
"running backwards/conroe to canarsie"
"open up/this is the police"

Late Summer *1990*

Sydné and I spend the afternoon with Shange at her home in Philadelphia. Shange explains the history of the poems, many of which are several years old. The love/sex poems, "even tho yr sampler broke down on you," "serial monogamy," "intermittent celibacy," "loosening strings or give me an 'A'," "m.e.s.l. (male english as a second language): in defense of bilingualism," "devotion from one lover to another" and "if i go all the way without you where would i go?" are all from a collection entitled *The Love Space Demands*. The gritty, reality-based poems, "i heard eric dolphy in his eyes," "crack annie," "open up/this is the police" and "running backwards/conroe to canarsie" are from a separate collection entitled *I Heard Eric Dolphy in His Eyes*. Shange also explains that many of these poems have been presented in performance with dance and music off and on for a period of two years.

Shange says that the poems represent the languages spoken by different kinds of people. Together the poems explore the languages of love and romance as well as that of the drug culture. She tells us that her thoughts have recently turned to the language of love in the age of AIDS. "Now, everybody's talking about what their T-cell count is. You never even heard of this stuff before a couple of years ago." Shange is considering writing additional poetry for the piece that will explore these themes and what she calls "t-cell language."

At our weekly breakfast meeting (Monday, September 8) we (Crossroads Artistic Director Ricardo Khan, Associate Producer Ken Johnson, Sydné and I) discuss possible directors. Since Genesis is also used as an opportunity to showcase the talents of Crossroads staff members, Sydné proposes writer/director Talvin Wilks. Talvin, whose play *Tod, the Boy, Tod* was produced by Crossroads the previous season, is currently the company's development coordinator. Ricardo is concerned that Talvin is too inexperienced to work with an artist of Shange's caliber. We remind him that that is the kind of opportunity Genesis was created to provide—a chance for emerging artists to develop their craft in a low pressure, yet professional environment. When we consult Shange, she's very receptive to the idea of working with someone new.

Sydné and Talvin go to Philadelphia to see Shange and musician/composer William "Spaceman" Patterson perform *The Love Space Demands* at the Painted Bride. The performance consists of Shange reading the poems accompanied by Spaceman on electric guitar.

Winter 1990

Shange (whom we all now call "Zake," short for Ntozake) and Spaceman come to Crossroads to discuss the development of the piece with Ricardo, Talvin, Sydné and me. As the poems have been performed before in one incarnation or another, and because there will be live music (performed by Spaceman) everyone agrees that *The Love Space Demands* deserves more than the usual twelve-hour Genesis rehearsal period. It is also agreed that because of Zake's popularity, *The Love Space Demands* will be presented more than once (also unusual for Genesis). Zake has asked that a long-time collaborator and friend, Mickey Davidson, be brought in to choreograph the work. Mickey was Zake's choreographer for a production of *I Heard Eric Dolphy in His Eyes* in California.

February 1991: Genesis project

Talvin explores the text for dramatic cohesiveness. He states his goal as being, "to create an environment which can support what Zake and Space have been doing with these poems . . . for this con-

Ezra Knight, Jackie Mari Roberts, William "Spaceman" Patterson, Ntozake Shange, Theara J. Ward and Demitri Corbin in The Love Space Demands. *Photograph by Rich Pipeling.*

text [Genesis]." With the exception of "irrepressibly bronze, beautiful & mine," all of the poems from the manuscript are to be performed in Genesis. The order of the pieces has been slightly altered so that "devotion from one lover to another" and "if i go all the way without you . . ." will end the performance on a romantic note.

Zake, who is familiar with the world of theatre as well as that of poetry, proves to be a great collaborator. She's very open to Talvin's explorations of the text and the order in which the poems are to be presented. Zake says her understanding of the necessities of the dramatic form is the reason she writes books. "I know how people need to change things in theatre—to make it work for the stage. As long as I've got my books and I know that somewhere in the universe what I wrote is the way I want it, I'm fine."

At this point, we discuss whether to create a "script" or to continue our use of the uncorrected manuscript proof. Talvin feels that a clean script would be helpful. Zake says that a clean script is fine, as long as "the words fall on the paper" the way she wrote them, i.e. the retyping of the text follows the word placement structure of the original poems. Each voice is distinct and the positions of the words on the page tell of multiplicity or singularity, naturalistic dialect or song, order or chaos.

Zake informs us that the flow of the language is what she uses to connect emotionally to each moment in performance. The poem "running backwards/conroe to canarsie," for example, changes voice and point of view. Divided into four movements, the poem begins as a first-person narrative that offers a personal overview of the history of racial incrimination of black men:

> before i was born
> they said/the Scottsboro Boys did it
> when/i was a child/
> they said/Emmett Till did it/
> now/i'ma woman/
> and my child's a child/
> and they say/Clarence Brandley did it/

The movement ends with the voice changing to that of a white mob:

> ask any/white man/in Conroe/
> Run, niggah, Run!
>
>   Got me a niggah this time.
> I got ya this time!
>
>   Can ya hear me, boy!
>
> Hey, Niggah!
>
>   Over here!

That's right, niggah.

Right here!

I been waitin' for this a long time.

The voice of the white mob continues through the second and third sections. Movement II begins with a first-person narrative:

> we's eatin' pizza at the pizza shop/
> when we see's these niggahs/at the
> counter talkin' like they's gonna eat
> some pizza too/

Movement III is a refrain of the mob attack that ends Movement I. The final movement returns us to the black community for comfort, and catharsis beginning with:

> hush now/don't explain
> there's nothin' to gain
> i'm glad you're back/
> don't explain

did you have a black boy for his neck to
be broke/for his father to see forsook
tell me/cuz i wanna know/

March 1991

Crossroads Production Manager Gary Kechely presents his design for the Genesis set. It is comprised of several black cubes, long flats, music stands and chairs that can be arranged according to the needs of the individual pieces. Each poem will have a distinct tone and motion. In addition to minimal set design, there is also a simple lighting plot designed by Dan Hochstine.

Talvin, Zake, Spaceman and Mickey Davidson begin a week-

long rehearsal process in preparation for Genesis. As presented in
the past, *The Love Space Demands* poems were read by Zake with
musical accompaniment by Spaceman. Talvin works to incorporate
Spaceman more organically into the poetry. In the context of the
"love space," he is her lover, and the object of her joy and confu-
sion. Many of the poems are now duets with Spaceman either
singing, speaking or playing his guitar to express a variety of relationships with Zake.

The dramatic action is more easily defined in the *Eric Dolphy*
poems because they were written as a choreopoem to be performed. The poem, "i heard eric dolphy in his eyes," for example,
is the narrative of a woman who, while waiting for a subway train,
witnesses the abuse of a homeless child by his father. She then sees
the father panhandling and excusing his actions with a simple, "ya
know how kids are/sometimes/ya gotta be a lil hard on em." Zake
is the witness telling us what she sees as she sees it; Spaceman is the
child's father, his guitar now an instrument used to coerce guilty
commuters into giving him money; and invisible at his side is the
battered child.

While there are no real dance numbers, every piece involves a
degree of choreographed movement. One task of Mickey's choreography is to facilitate interaction between Zake and Spaceman, who
has a limited range of motion because of his electric guitar.

The Love Space Demands opens the Genesis festival on March
13, 1991, followed by performances on March 14 and 16. The audience response for all three performances is extremely positive.
While many audience members admit to needing some time to get
into the rhythm of the piece, most say that they were involved by
"i heard eric dolphy in his eyes." Questions from the audience go
beyond inquiries into the evolution of *The Love Space Demands*.
People are interested in Zake's other works (many women admit
that *for colored girls* was a personal watershed in their lives). When
asked who influenced her work, Zake says:

Brecht was a perfect example, to me, of how a poet can function in the theatre. . . . As a poet, I also knew, not unlike García Lorca, that because we are poets, we have to find the form again for ourselves; that we don't come to the theatre as a theatre person—we come as language people. So we come hearing something and then we have to think of a character to say it, as opposed to the way I think a lot of playwrights write. They have the characters and then they have to figure out how that person talks. . . . Brecht was [also] meaningful to me in a sense that he was able to find dignity in people in whom we thought that there was nothing—that there could be nothing after all this. And that was important to me because growing up looking at stereotypes of black, Latin and Asian people all my life, you would think that we were nothing already; I knew that wasn't true.

When asked about the development of the music (did he use existing music from some of the many composers and musicians mentioned in the poems?), Spaceman replies that the music for each poem was developed specifically for this production. He didn't want just to provide "musical phrases" for every named musician or song, he wanted to "do with the music what Zake did with the words," pay tribute to those artists while creating something original at the same time.

Presenting *The Love Space Demands* showed us that our traditional theatregoing audience could enjoy a foray into the radically different. And Zake feels that she has found a true collaborator in Talvin and an artistic home in Crossroads.

Ricardo wants very much to do a main-stage project with Zake but questions whether *Love Space* is the one to choose. Can *The Love Space Demands* be sold as part of a subscription series and

The ensemble in the scene "intermittent celibacy." Photograph by Rich Pipeling.

survive the grueling eight performances a week for six weeks? Is there a large enough audience for Zake's work in this area (New Brunswick, New Jersey)? How would we market it and to whom? Do these poems have the same dramatic energy and clarity as *for colored girls* and *Spell #7*, which were enjoyed by mass audiences?

There are also the rigors of a two-person performance piece to be considered. This kind of work is tough on both the audience and the two people who must carry an entire evening. There is also the pressure of creating a theatrical "production." Too few design elements could cause an audience to question whether they're getting their money's worth; too many could overwhelm the performers.

Talvin's inexperience as a director also concerns Ricardo. While Genesis has, from time to time, provided all of us with the opportunity to work as artists and to do something outside of our administrative duties, the final product has rarely been transferred to the main stage. It's one thing to support collaboration between a young director and an established artist like Zake in what amounts to a lab situation, and quite another to entrust the development of a new work, the pressures of an audience and critics, to a novice.

Despite his doubts, Ricardo decides to include *The Love Space Demands* in Crossroads' 1991–92 season and to support Zake's desire to have Talvin as her director.

Zake, Spaceman, Talvin and Mickey form a collaborative core that Zake names the "Lunar Unit."

Spring 1991

Now that the piece is to become a production, the first issue is whether it is enough to have Zake and Spaceman perform alone. Does the text lend itself credibly to other voices? Are Spaceman and Zake characters in a world or are they the entire world? Another concern is that Spaceman's musical presence during Genesis was often more dominant than an accompaniment. This, combined with his speaking lines, tended to cause Spaceman to overshadow Zake in performance. The imbalance made it difficult to decide on whom to focus.

Ricardo wants other performers used so that the language can be better dramatized. He wants more narrative and character-ization and for Spaceman's role to be clearly and exclusively musi-cal. Zake's concern is that, as a performer, her ability to relate to the world she's created will be severely impaired by the creation of characters with names:

> I didn't want these particular poems taken from me and made into some fictional person's poems. . . . I didn't like the dislocation I had with pieces in *for colored girls* or *Spell #7*, where people would ask me

about these characters and I didn't know what they
were talking about because the names were so artificial to me. . . . I had put names on them because they
had to have characters and have names. I don't remember who they are, and I don't like not remembering my
work because it was made away from me.

It has also been almost twenty years since Zake last performed as part of an ensemble. Her skills as a poet/performance
artist are fine, but in the context of a production where she'll be
asked to sing, dance and act, again, there are doubts as to her ability to carry it off. During her Genesis performances there were
moments when she could not be understood clearly by the audiences—not because of volume, but because of the way she enun-
ciates certain words.

For their part, members of the Lunar Unit question Crossroads' commitment to them and the project. Contracts have not
been forthcoming and there has been little discussion about the way
in which the piece is expected to develop. At the heart of things is
Zake's desire to present this piece as a solo performance.

Talvin is caught between his long association with Crossroads as producer and his new role as director supporting and collaborating with a brilliant writer/performer. To Talvin's mind, however, the world could be opened up more. There are more voices
to be heard than two. There is also the need for dance (as well as
Spaceman's music) and for visual images.

Summer 1991

Talvin meets photographer Adál Maldonato. Talvin has been thinking all along about adding a visual component to the production.
Until meeting Adál, he thought of using a variety of different pho-

tographers, but after seeing Adál's work, Talvin now feels that Adál is the perfect choice. His black-and-white images have humor and a certain literal quality. He is, also, a long-time friend of Zake's who was already doing a photo series of her. The photographs that Adál has already taken (some of which are erotic nudes) will become the basis for the visual world. The idea is to recreate Zake's spirit visually as well as textually.

August 1991

Talvin and I meet for lunch at the Frog and the Peach for an update. Talvin had requested time to workshop the piece. Through the theatre's African-American College Initiative Program (AACIP), this season he will travel to seven historically black colleges in the southeast and develop the piece by working with student actors. However, before he can begin that process, he needs to work with the bodies and voices of professional performers here at home. I give him the news that Crossroads has set his workshop for September 23–27.

At this point, Talvin is considering an ensemble of five: Zake, Spaceman, one male dancer, one female dancer and one actor "who can move." In response to Ricardo's concern about cohesiveness, the Lunar Unit has developed a possible narrative through-line and created a theatrical context for the poems. The self-named Lunar Unit, now also including Adál, is exploring the possiblity of setting *The Love Space Demands* on the moon. As Talvin says, "It's sort of like putting *Spell #7* in a bar; anything can happen." A character Zake created called Lieutenant Commander Paradise will act as our guide through the world of the "love space." The character is based on a short story that Zake wrote about a mad scientist who wants to destroy the moon. The premise of the story is that the destruction of the moon would also end all things physical (menstrual flow and tides) and metaphysical (love, romance, lunacy) associated with the moon.

The idea of the moon as a landscape for *The Love Space Demands* was also inspired by Samuel Delany's erotic science fiction novel, *Stars in My Pocket Like Grains of Sand*. The novel has provided the group with a futuristic landscape for dealing with sexuality and gender. In the book, pronouns like "he" or "she" when describing a relationship do not necessarily refer to male or female. A "he/she" relationship can exist between two men or two women. "He/she" refers to certain dynamics of power and energy that all beings possess and respect. Delany also creates a society that accepts sexual combinations beyond male/female monogamy. The Lunar Unit feels, according to Talvin, that "the book is a science-fiction articulation of what *The Love Space Demands* can be." The group is attempting to create a context for the work and to provide Zake with a character who, while not Zake, is organic to Zake and in sync with her way of looking at this world.

I question whether the creation of such a premise (Lt. Comdr. Paradise as our lunar tour guide) will really add clarity to the world of *The Love Space Demands* or whether it will be just another element for an audience to have to work through? Is this the dramatic anchor we've been looking for? How would the other characters, then, be introduced? Who are they? Talvin envisions a collage of dance, text and projections dealing (not necessarily literally) with the themes of the poems: "The Lt. Comdr. Paradise reality would be woven in and connected to those same issues."

Talvin has begun looking at the poems in groups as a series of movements. The first three poems ("even tho yr sampler broke down on you," "serial monogamy" and "intermittent celibacy") comprise the first movement entitled "The Landing." This segment "takes us to the moon." The poems reflect Lt. Comdr. Paradise's fantasies involving love and sex. Talvin anticipates these poems will be recorded and the poetry will be played against a

visual backdrop of nude photos of Zake reclining on a couch jux-
taposed with images of space and Earth. This first sequence will also
introduce the players by means of a dance sequence. "Serial
monogamy" will explore the relationship between Zake as the lead
character and each of three men (Spaceman and two male performers). "Intermittent celibacy" is an exchange between Zake and
the other woman in the ensemble, who represents the other side
of Zake's character, so that the poem takes the form of a conversation with one's self. Talvin wants the voices to work the way the
poems work: "They should have a dreamlike quality."

The second movement features "m.e.s.l. (male english as a
second language): in defense of bilingualism." The recitation of the
poem will be accompanied by a photo series of Zake as a boxer.
Images of an elegant couple dancing in a gym will be woven
between images from old black-and-white movies and images of
boxing as a "symbolic expression of the poem." Beginning at this
point, the lunar theme makes no sense to me. The world is clearly
an earthbound one and the moon makes no difference here at all.

The same is true of the third movement, which is comprised
of "i heard eric dolphy in his eyes," "crack annie" and "running
backwards/conroe to canarsie." At this point, "i heard eric dolphy
in his eyes" will be staged as a group scene with projections of sub-
ways and people, and be more dance oriented. "Crack annie" is a
shadow dance that will interpret the action of a child's rape. Talvin
plans for Zake to recite the poem in front of a screen; the images
will grow larger behind her. "Running backward/conroe to
canarsie" will rely more on a photo collage than the onstage action.
The piece will feature documentary footage of lynchings and
white mobs from Canarsie and Bensonhurst. The photo series will
feature Zake holding a flaming newspaper. The intent is to show
that mob violence against blacks has been occurring for centuries
and that there is no difference between the violence then and the
violence now.

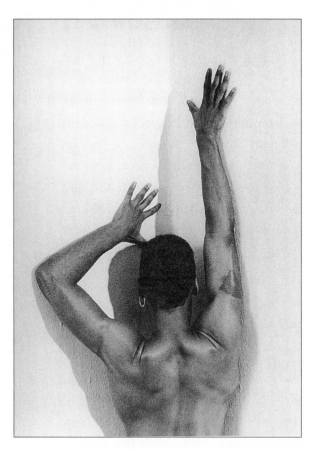

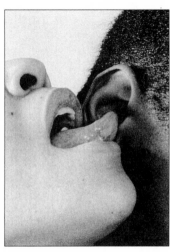

Slide projection photographs by Adál.

The final poem that Talvin outlines is "if i go all the way without you where would i go?" He sees that as a choral piece.

Zake plans to write a T-cell poem as well as additional material to aid the transitions of the moon theme. I expect a new draft of the script by Labor Day. Talvin wants to consider Loy Arcenas for the set design and Heather Carson, a lighting designer from the world of dance, whose work Talvin has seen recently. At this point he has no clue who should do the costumes, but he shows me some pictures he cut out of a magazine of little leather-thonged and lycra outfits.

September 1991

Talvin has to cast the workshop from our files. There isn't a lot of time. Zake recommends a young performer she's worked with named Claude Sloane. Talvin casts Isaiah Washington as his "actor." Talvin decides to add another woman, thus expanding the ensemble to six so that Zake and Spaceman can be a couple (he wants to explore the workings of couples). Dancer/actress Stephanie Berry and dancer Rasha-Mella round out the workshop cast.

Before going into the workshop we all have another focus meeting at Crossroads. Zake, Mickey, Spaceman, Sydné, Ricardo, Talvin and I participate. Zake begins the process by distributing copies of a Stephan Bodian interview with Sam Keen, entitled, "Do Men Drive Us to War?" (*Yoga Journal*, May/June 1991) in which Keen challenges us all to let go of "cherished assumptions about what it means to be a man"; another article from the same journal about the emerging men's movement; and a single, typed page with the words, "Thoughts for Meditations—Love Space Demands Core Unit" handwritten on the top. This page, which features excerpts from Octavio Paz's essay entitled "The Verbal Contract," begins:

In the beginning, poetry was oral: the word spoken before an audience. Or more exactly, recited or declaimed. The association between poetry, music and dance goes very far back in time; the three arts were probably born together and perhaps poetry was originally the word sung and danced ...

Zake wants to give us all a way of entering her world and she is clarifying why music and dance are as prominent as text. By sharing articles by men that discuss the need to explore and attempt to understand the nature of their brutality, Zake is also giving us a means for addressing her detractors, those who have criticized her work as being "anti-male." Zake also states her willingness to give up all her roles to other actors as long as she can keep "crack annie," which, to date, is the only monologue. The workshop draft of the script has been developed by Talvin. The poems have been divided into lines for an ensemble whose character names are simply: Man 1 (Spaceman), Man 2 (Isaiah), Man 3 (Claude), Woman 1 (Zake), Woman 2 (Stephanie), and Woman 3 (Rasha-Mella). There is no additional material from Zake, and the Lt. Comdr. Paradise idea, while not entirely abandoned, has remained undeveloped. But the structure of beginning the theatrical journey with Zake and introducing the other performers through music and erotic movement remains intact.

Since there is so little time, Talvin wants to focus on the other voices in the poems. For the purpose of getting through the week, he will explore only "serial monogamy," "intermittent celibacy," "third generation geechee myth for yr birthday," "i heard eric dolphy in his eyes," "crack annie," "running backwards/conroe to canarsie" and "open up/this is the police." It's doubtful that he'll get through them all, but that's the plan.

Talvin outlines his agenda for the upcoming week. The first day would be textual exploration with the core collaborators

(Talvin, Zake, Spaceman, Mickey and Adál). Actors will be added on the second day. Designers will come in on the third day. The fourth day will be strictly designers, since Zake has to teach and will be out of town that day. The fifth and final day will feature everyone and (hopefully) include a run-through of the week's work. We are also informed that New Jersey Network may be in on that day to film the process for an upcoming segment on their arts program.

Since the use of slides is going to be so important to the look of the set, everyone agrees that we should add a professional projectionist to the design team. Crossroads' Production Manager Gary Kechely recommends Anton Nelessen, a professional architect and environmental designer. Nelessen did the slides for Crossroads' world premiere production of George Wolfe's *The Colored Museum* and won the Hollywood Drama-Logue for his work on the show at the Mark Taper Forum.

Talvin also decides that he wants to employ costume designer Toni-Leslie James, who designed *Tod, the Boy, Tod* at Crossroads as well as George Wolfe's plays *Spunk* (at Crossroads and at the Mark Taper Forum) and *Jelly's Last Jam* (at the Taper and on Broadway). Toni hasn't accepted the offer yet.

Talvin's AACIP dates will begin right after the professional workshop. Starting October 3, he will be visiting four schools in October, two in November and one in April. The AACIP circuit will take him to North and South Carolina, Georgia, Virginia, Florida and the District of Columbia.

During the course of the workshop, Talvin arranges and rearranges groups of women, groups of men and couples. The watch word is "sex." Everyone is encouraged to touch, play, arouse and be aroused during the exploration of the first poems. The company's ability to improvise is especially necessary. Through this exploration, Talvin discovers that his initial instinct for "serial monogamy" was correct. The poem works with Zake involved with the three men. "Intermittent celibacy" becomes Zake talking to the other women, but the women aren't aspects of Zake's character (as Talvin had originally envisioned); they are her friends. Through the improvs for "intermittent celibacy," the men strike poses. Talvin sees them as objects in a "hunk museum" that the women are admiring like works of art.

For some of the poems, Spaceman's music seems to dictate the way they will be approached physically. His gospel-like riffs for "running backwards/conroe to canarsie" inspire Talvin to march out the ensemble like a church choir and to have them say the opening lines as if they're testifying to their faith. There are also some serious hard-rock guitar riffs that evoke the feeling of white kids hanging out and talking tough. In other poems, it's Mickey's choreography that leads the way. In "open up/this is the police," for example, the performers' entrances and exits, where they move and how, are designed by Mickey.

Through the course of the week, Talvin manages to shape the opening segments: "serial monogamy," "intermittent celibacy," "i heard eric dolphy in his eyes," "running backwards/conroe to canarsie" and "open up/this is the police."

On the "designer day," we all meet Anton "Tony" Nelessen and his assistant, Richard Carroll, who present rough drawings of possible screen configurations based on an earlier phone conversation between Tony and Talvin. Adál presents rough drawings that offer us some idea of the photographic sequences that will accompany each poem. Toni-Leslie James has expressed interest in the project, but is unable to attend the workshop. Heather needs a sense of how literally or symbolically she should approach the poems. Is "i heard eric dolphy in his eyes" literally in a subway station? If so, then the look of the sequence needs to stay dark. She also needs to consider the balance between lighting the performers and not washing out the slides.

The week ends with a run-through of the work done thus

Slide projection photograph by Adál.

far. The ensemble works well together and Talvin has invited them all to audition for the production in January.

December 1991

We hold a designers' meeting that includes Talvin, Heather, Adál, Tony Nelessen and Rich Carroll. Since the workshop, the theatre has moved from its old building on Memorial Parkway into a new home on Livingston Avenue. This meeting will also be an opportunity for the designers to see the new space so that they can revise their designs and budgets accordingly.

Based on their initial workshop presentation, Talvin decides that Tony and his assistant, Rich, will design the environment. The choice makes perfect sense given the significance of Adál's photographic images to the design of the set, and because no other designer whom Talvin trusts to do this show is available. Both Tony and Rich are architects and both understand clearly the world that Talvin is trying to create. In addition, Tony has worked in theatre before, and more important, he has worked at Crossroads before.

Talvin wants the world of this production to consist of: a lunar space; the cosmos and celestial spheres; symbolic representations of urban decay; and some sort of ancient ruins from no particular time or culture to show that the poems exist in perpetual time. Perhaps, Talvin suggests, a celestial map could be projected on the floor's surface.

Tony's four sketches include all of the elements that Talvin has requested, but according to Tony, "they are more symbolic than literal." Four beams will represent urban decay. Designed in an *L*-shaped pattern, placed vertically on the stage, they will be brick red (inspired by the old Crossroads). They will also house the four-member band who will accompany Spaceman musically. The band will be stationed on a platform and will be visible to the audience. A pillared temple will be used for actors' entrances and exits.

Six veils, hanging from the grid, each on different planes with one large screen in the back will be used as projection surfaces. Each screen can be adjusted to various levels or rolled up completely. Dancers can also go between screens. The screen sizes can be adjusted to insure that the projected images don't overwhelm the performers—twelve feet is the maximum length of each.

Adál asks if the screens could be tracked so that they move backward and forward as well as up and down. His idea for "i heard eric dolphy in his eyes" includes "a series of shots of a subway train that look like they're coming towards the audience." Other shots he has planned rely on the screens' ability to fracture images and give the illusion of depth. Tony says that he can design some of the screens to be attached to rollers on a separate track.

Heather mentions the possible difficulty of lighting people in front of the screens. Lights bright enough to show the actors may wash out the projected images. A choice may have to be made between seeing the actor and seeing the image. Tony suggests using a black scrim to catch the spill. Heather believes that would make the images "clean and prim" and that's not what any of them wants.

Heather also cautions that the color of the veils and the set will affect her ability to light the space. Since Adál's photographs will be black and white, Tony can design the projection veils to be black. But, he warns, if the veils are black, only whites and greys will show through. Heather is most concerned about the dark pillars and the black background of the set design. Adál adds that he also wants to be able to project words onto the veils, like "Run, Niggah, Run" in the "running backwards/conroe to canarsie" sequence.

Tony's ancient ruins will be sandstone, green, red and gold. They will have Egyptian characters and, if necessary, they can be structurally sound enough for the performers to dance on. The consensus is that instead of Egyptian characters, other icons and symbols could be incorporated on the ruins, so that they won't seem so specific. Heather and Talvin would also like for the colors of the set to be lost, occasionally, and replaced by stark black and white to provide another kind of dramatic emphasis. As the design develops, the group will have to talk more. To make all the stage visuals work, they must communicate and find areas of compromise.

Talvin presents the third draft of the script, informing us that further script revisions will have more to do with vocal assignments than text. This draft is closer to a production draft and includes stage directions for how the images are expected to work as well as the music. The piece has been divided into two acts.

ACT I
introduction (an abridged version of the introduction to the
    book, *The Love Space Demands*, done as a voice-over)
"even tho yr sampler broke down on you"
"serial monogamy"
"intermittent celibacy"
"a third generation geechee myth for yr birthday"
"i heard eric dolphy in his eyes"
"m.e.s.l. (male english as a second language): in defense of
    bilingualism"

ACT II
"running backwards/conroe to canarsie"
"crack annie"
"open up/this is the police"
"devotion from one lover to another"
"if i go all the way without you where would i go?"

The poem "loosening strings or give me an 'A' " was cut from the piece. Talvin has absolutely no idea where to put it or how to dramatize it.

In a script meeting, Talvin and I talk about what, if any, structure exists. The Aristophanic model could be loosely applied, with the romantic and fun-natured poems giving way to the harsher, more reality-based poems that flow into a denouement (of sorts) with the return to romantic poetry. Rather than force the whole into some model that was never made to suit it, however, Talvin commits to making the moments of each individual poem live. Together, they form a world of love and violence, decay and renewal. This last look at the order of the poems convinces us that there is enough of a dramatic through-line to engage an audience.

Talvin, Mickey, Spaceman and Zake audition actors with Maria Nelson and Ellen Marshall of Orpheus Group, Inc. on December 10. Ricardo and I join them on December 12 for callbacks. From the pool of twenty-one performers called back, the four selections are virtually unanimous: former Living Stage Theatre Company member Ezra Knight; dancer/actress Theara Ward; recent Yale acting graduate Jackie Mari Roberts; and Demitri Corbin, a young, Chicago-born actor and playwright. They are all physically different with different strengths and complementary abilities (Ezra, athletic; Theara, graceful; Jackie, vulnerable; Demitri, sensitive). All are good actors with some ability to move.

The rehearsal period has been broken up because Zake, Talvin and Spaceman will be presenting *The Love Space Demands* as a one-woman performance piece in January at the Lorraine Hansberry Theatre in San Francisco. This small production will give Talvin one last chance to hear the poems in the draft form that we'll be using for rehearsal. There will be four days of rehearsal from January 21-23. Rehearsals will resume on February 4, with the first preview scheduled for February 27.

Adál begins shooting erotic/love pictures featuring Zake, Mickey and Isaiah Washington.

January 21–23, 1992

First phase of rehearsals for *The Love Space Demands*. Talvin's goals for this week are:

1) To flesh out material
2) To integrate performers into the process
3) To touch on all the group pieces and find the dynamics of the ensemble

The performing ensemble is joined by musicians Dengal Warren Benbow (drums and synth drums) and Osborne "Dinky" Bingham (keyboards and background vocals).

The first day includes a production/concept meeting. Each Crossroads production is prefaced by such a meeting, which is used to orient the company about the goals and processes of the production. To discuss *The Love Space Demands*, Talvin offers an overview of the rehearsal process. Zake talks about the history of the piece as poems and her performances of several of them. She also talks about her collaborative history with Mickey, Spaceman and Adál, all of whom she has known and worked with for at least ten years. Spaceman talks about performing with Zake and composing the music for the poems. Rich Carroll presents blueprints and the model for the set and explains the physical world in which the production will live. That world will include nine rectangular, hanging screens on which the images will be projected. Each screen will have the flexibility to be raised and lowered and will be integrated into each performance segment.

After the first day, Talvin and Mickey realize that they need to get together at the beginning of each day to plan their day's work before they are joined by the cast. Each day's work is videotaped and reviewed at the end of the day by Talvin, Mickey and Spaceman. Talvin then goes home and maps out the directions for the next day. By the second day, Talvin's "challenge" becomes apparent: "to maintain spontaneity while incorporating structure." The performers do great improv work, but when it's time for the physicality and energy of the improvs to be incorporated with saying the text and singing, they lose their focus.

The first part of each rehearsal begins with everyone (including the stage managers and me) warming up together. Then the acting ensemble goes downstairs with Mickey for movement devoted to the poem to be explored that day. While they're moving, the band is practicing in the rehearsal hall—Spaceman has composed most of the music, but he's still exploring chords and instrumentation. The second part of the day is spent with Talvin (a former student of Living Stage alum Tina Shepard; Paul Zimet; and Jean-Claude van Itallie) leading the actors in improvisational exercises to music. The exercises encourage the performers to create individual characters for each poem. At the end of the day, Talvin attaches the day's work to that of the previous day and tries to work out transitions. He is working the poems in the order they are laid out in the script.

At the end of the three days, Talvin and Mickey get a sense of "each performer's physical vocabulary." They also manage to do substantial work on the first three pieces ("sampler," "serial monogamy" and "intermittent celibacy"). By the third day, we are joined for the first time by Sound Designer Carmen Whiip. Carmen spends much of the day with Spaceman, talking about his equipment and what he wants to achieve. Carmen is the perfect choice—not only is she a professional theatre sound designer, but she is a musician and a member of a professional band, IBIS. She is the perfect bridge between Talvin and Spaceman.

Talvin ends the first three days of rehearsal by encouraging the performers to read the text with no thought of how the voices in the poems are to be divided. They are to read to understand the world of each poem.

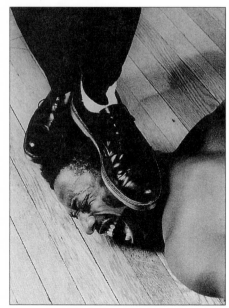

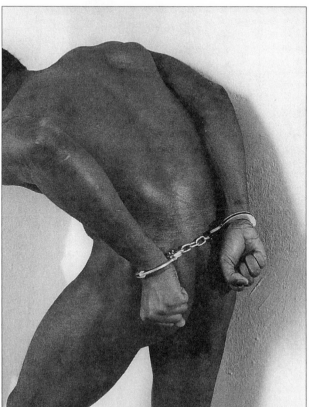

*Director Talvin Wilks
(top left). All slide
projection photographs
by Adál.*

January 24–February 2

Talvin, Zake and Space present *The Love Space Demands* at the Lorraine Hansberry Theatre.

February 4–9

The cast and collaborators have been reassembled. Since the set is so unusual (ramps, screens and unusual angles), Talvin spends a lot of time walking actors through the taped rehearsal hall. It's important that they understand that there will be definite barriers. Stage Manager Patreshettarlini Adams supplies everyone with maps of the stage so that the performers can record their own blocking. I provide Talvin and the performers with a glossary of terms used in the poems as well as a set of tapes that music historian Robert LaPierre has made of the songs and musicians mentioned in the poems.

This week's work includes beginning explorations of "a third generation geechee myth for yr birthday," "running backwards/conroe to canarsie," "devotion from one lover to another," "open up/this is the police" and "if i go all the way without you where would i go?" We are joined for the first time by Costume Designer Toni-Leslie James. She's currently designing the costumes for *Jelly's Last Jam* on Broadway, so we'll be relying a lot on her assistant, Leslie McGovern.

Spaceman is having a problem making several lines work musically:

> cuz/we done come careenin out severely colored
> stratospheres/
> surgin with the force of them/what
> am in the tradition/& them what ain't

The actors have to sing it so quickly that it doesn't flow and you can't understand what they're saying; the musical phrasing is also extremely awkward. After looking at it, Zake and Space change it to:

cuz we done come careening out severely colored stratospheres/
surgin' with the force of tradition what am and what ain't.

February 11–16

This week included the designer run-through. Absent, however, were Toni-Leslie James and Tony Nelessen. Adál arrived halfway through. This week everyone had blow-ups. Zake didn't want me in rehearsal anymore. Since the text is completed, what was my purpose? According to Talvin, Zake believes everyone else in the room is contributing in the moment to the development of the piece while the bulk of my work (assisting Talvin in shaping the order and division of voices of the poems) was done before rehearsals started, and the next biggest part of my contribution (production notes) won't begin until previews. Zake needs to know that I'm not merely this presence that's sitting around and secretly criticizing the work that's going on. Talvin explained to Zake my role in documenting the process. She immediately relented. For my part, I won't attend rehearsals so frequently. I've never had to deal with this kind of hostility before, and I feel that the best way to cope with this level of anxiety is to be as clear as I can about every minute I plan to spend in the process. I try to make sure at the beginning of each day that Zake and Talvin know if I am going to be in rehearsal and why. The process of creating a production from a book is a new one for me (as it is for all of us except Zake) and documenting the evolution of this piece is my function for the

Slide projection photographs by
Adál.

theatre. At the same time, I do understand Zake's vulnerability. This is the first time that she has worked as part of a performing ensemble since *for colored girls* in 1973. Nothing is more important than making her feel protected and comfortable. She still has a lot of work ahead of her.

Adál has shot all of the photos horizontally, nothing was shot vertically, which means that Tony's long, rectangular projection veils cannot be used singularly—they must all be used in sets of three. Tony wants Adál to reshoot but Adál has spent his entire budget shooting and developing the first set of pictures. Heather can't design the lights without first seeing how the slides are going to look, so she's already behind. The opening montage voice-over was held up for hours while Audio Supervisor Dan Hochstine and Spaceman argued over recording levels. And our stage manager's grandmother passed away, so she's going to have to go to North Carolina after rehearsal on Saturday for the funeral. Zake, Spaceman, Adál, Mickey and Talvin have worked together so closely and for so long that it's hard for the other designers to feel a part of the "collaborative spirit." Spaceman with Dan and Carmen; Adál with Tony and Heather are examples of the difficulty the original collaborators are having relating to their new partners. Spaceman is a musician and Adál a professional visual artist, so many of their problems result from their relative inexperience in making what they do work for theatre. Talvin is so focused on the actors now that he has no time to ease the transitions of his Lunar Unit collaborators. When we move into the theatre, he'll devote more time to those elements of the production.

Mickey's choreography for "open up/this is the police" and "a third generation geechee myth for yr birthday" is the toughest for the performers to get a handle on, especially for Jackie, who is not a dancer. Even Theara, who is a dancer, is baffled by some of this stuff. If they can't get it together when we move into the theatre, Mickey will simplify it.

Zake has requested a diction coach and I'm looking into it. She's showing a genuine desire to become performance ready. She's about to blow a blood vessel over the ensemble's Spanish pronunciations, so I'm looking into a Spanish dialect coach to work with them on "open up/this is the police." Zake is continually frustrated by the way the other actors say things. Now, she objects to the way Demitri says, "i heard eric dolphy in his eyes." A big part of the problem is that no one understands the profundity of Zake's words in the same way that she does. When asked to clarify the meaning of the line "i heard/eric dolphy in his eyes/," she tells us what a great musician he was and how he had a ridge across his forehead that reminded her of a unicorn's horn. Also, his death was so sudden and occurred at such a young age, she began to see him as something mythical. So when she writes about seeing Eric Dolphy in the eyes of an abused and battered boy "who has mastered the art of weepin & smilin/at the same time," she means not only music but also the mythical presence of who Dolphy was to her as a teenager. We can get the Spanish pronunciations right, I can provide a glossary of terms, and they can listen to Dolphy's saxophone solos until they're deaf, but only she can provide the kind of insight into her words that speaks to the different levels on which she writes.

Once Zake asked me to ask her why Crack Annie's daughter was named "Berneatha." "Zake, why is Crack Annie's daughter named Berneatha?"

"Because, it's supposed to be Beneatha like in *A Raisin in the Sun*—that's a family drama too."

Zake has made it clear that since she is performing, she doesn't want to be involved in production meetings. She says that we all know by now how she feels and if we don't, Mickey certainly does and has her proxy. She also does not want to be constantly approached about textual references, even though when asked she does respond.

Talvin works with the performers individually this week to

help them develop specificity of character and make distinct choices about who they are in each poem.

Ezra has asked if he could add American sign language to his physical vocabulary for "devotion from one lover to another." It's a good idea since Talvin wants the piece to be an exploration of the language of love. Talvin has some notion of how he wants to stage the poem, but it's not really clear to him, so he can't really clarify it to the company. At the heart of it is Ezra presented as an object of desire for Jackie, Theara and Demitri.

February 18–23

We went onto the set this week. Talvin is insisting that the performers make definitive choices. Since Zake is here, company members are so afraid of being wrong in their interpretations that they're not doing anything consistently. It's as if they're looking for her approval more than the director's.

Talvin's original blocking and Mickey's choreography hold up well in the theatre, but we're still waiting for the veils.

Since the performers have different theatrical experiences, some adapt more easily than others to Talvin's process and the nature of creating this piece. Ezra, for example, is a former member of the Living Stage Theatre Company of Washington, D.C., so his process fits comfortably with Talvin's Chaikin-inspired technique. Jackie, who received her MFA from the Yale School of Drama, tends to be not too responsive the first day a new idea is presented to her, but comes back the next day with some interesting character ideas. Demitri and Theara are the proverbial hard workers. They tackle every task with earnest concentration and enthusiasm. They make new choices again and again. While their ability to adapt is wonderful, their reluctance to commit to one idea for more than a day sets them back.

We can't agree on whether or not to include a glossary of terms in the playbill. Due to limited space, it would have to be an abridged version of what was given to the actors. Zake doesn't want it to go in unless it can explain the intellectual and symbolic places that her words are coming from, not just their denotative meanings. For example, in "open up/this is the police" the words "mira! mira!" mean literally, "Look! Look!," but in the context in which she places them, they are also an untranslatable exclamatory phrase shouted and accompanied by a single raised fist during liberation rallies in Latin America. Talvin has adopted an "I don't care if they don't understand" attitude, feeling that if the power of the production isn't enough to give people some intuitive understanding of what they're seeing, then he's failed anyway and no glossary is going to help.

Zake begins working with Dialect Coach Lynda Gravatt. Talvin also uses this week to block the introduction of the performers with Mickey's help.

Some basic redesign work has to be done to the set, as well. Warren's platform needs to be elevated (he's positioned so low that he can't see Spaceman give him cues). The muslin veils are so flimsy that they crinkle easily and won't roll up all the way. Their current design of two long strips sewn together at the center causes an hour-glass type of pucker. By Saturday, the slides still aren't sequenced. Act II has not even been loaded. On Sunday the computer doing the sequencing crashes and everything has to be loaded again.

February 24–March 1

Zake's introduction in the book provides a clear understanding of how she came to write these poems. The book's intro has been edited and recorded by Zake. Instead of music, her recorded voice, modulated by Spaceman and Carmen, is the sound that accompanies the performers' entrances.

The first preview is February 27. Everyone's tense. Previews are followed by post-show discussions and then meetings with Ricardo.

The meetings in Ricardo's office after these first previews consist mostly of technical notes. Among them are Sydné's observation that the images for "devotion from one lover to another" were supposed to include flowers and water images. Instead they're all phallic (smoke stacks, trains etc.). We also discuss the audience's post-show comments about not being able to hear the actors over the music. In addition, they say it's difficult to see the performers without washing out the slides. Tony will sequence the images sooner, so that they can be seen clearly during the transitions between poems. Then they'll fade away so the lights can be directed more fully on the actors when it's time for them to speak. The sound is a constant problem because everything that Carmen does in the booth, Spaceman undoes from his controls on the stage. As it stands, no one can hear "i heard eric dolphy in his eyes." Zake's costume for the close of the show is all wrong and most unflattering. The audience, as predicted, is having a difficult time deciding where to focus. Problems vary according to where in the house one sits. Due to the fragmentation of the images, the dark lighting and stage configuration, not every seat is a good one. But the first preview ends with a standing ovation. Zake proves to be an exciting and charismatic performer and the ensemble looks and sounds great (when you can hear them).

March 2–7

The battles wage on. Lighting becomes better, but the look of the show remains dark. The sound balance is never right throughout.

Even though the performers are wearing body mics, it's still hard to modulate them to be heard over the music. When they're turned up too loud, there's static feedback.

The more the ensemble performs, the more layered their performances become. All of the performers are discovering their voices.

While audience response varies from favorable to a few walk-outs at intermission, we see the project as a triumph. As for me, I cannot imagine a tougher or more exciting production to end my tenure at Crossroads. I have been offered and have accepted a job in the literary/dramaturgy department at the Lincoln Center Theater in New York.

Ricardo challenged the Crossroads staff and audience to explore the styles and ways in which our work can manifest itself. While as an institution we were accomplished in the craft of play-making, when charged with helping to create something totally different, we had to shake off old models and discover new ones. According to Ricardo, "Challenging pre-existing forms and breaking through the lines, this is what theatre is; this is what Zake's all about. She dared to venture into a place that is as scary, dangerous and wonderful as love is, and we were part of the development of a new vocabulary for love."

Sometime after the run of the show, I asked Zake to comment on her experience with *The Love Space Demands*. The following were her thoughts on the process:

> I am so glad to be working/writing today, the fortieth anniversary of Fidel Castro's raid on the Mancado Barracks, because just as that battle did not "win" that war, the battle defined and inspired a conception of the world that had not existed before. In the same way Crossroads Theatre allowed me and my associates to reach some grounds/visions we'd never tapped before.

Author Ntozake Shange. Slide projection photograph by Adál.

Originally, as always, *The Love Space Demands* was a series of sculpted poems not unlike *for colored girls*, in the sense that both pieces began in intimate non-theatrical, choreographic and non-narrative environments. The poems (monologues) in *The Love Space Demands* are, to me, no different than those in *for colored girls*. Yet it seems to me that the general public (whoever that is) had an easier time with *for colored girls* than *The Love Space Demands*. The reason for this discrepancy (since I am still me) has to do with several areas which only aesthetics, politics and flexibility define.

First of all, we (Talvin Wilks, director; Mickey Davidson, choreographer; and William "Spaceman" Patterson, composer) came to Crossroads as a unit, which meant that Crossroads' creative input would be secondary to ours. Secondly, I required as much time for music and dance rehearsals as I did for the so-called "text" exposition, which inflated our budget and that of technical personnel immensely. The last dilemma we confronted was that I, Zake, was performing in the piece and therefore could not see or hear anything the director, choreographer, composer or sound designer was doing!

The only reasons *The Love Space Demands* worked as beautifully as it did was because: (1) My associates and I had done a lot of work on the poems, their sequence and intensity, before we got to Crossroads (for no less than a year and a half across the country); (2) I had and have intense working relationships with Mickey D., Spaceman and Talvin, so we always knew what we wanted from each other; (3) To its credit and that of Rick Khan, Sydné Mahone and

Shelby Jiggetts, Crossroads Theatre supported us on every level conceivable.

We were allowed a substantial workshop in the fall before our opening, where the text could be changed, rearranged or cut as we saw fit. This was a remarkable and substantive gift because a lot (almost all) of my light cues were based on the score and movement as opposed to the "language." In addition, Crossroads supplied us with what turned out to be a very expensive visual environment, created by Adál with flies, slides, lifts, etc. (by Tony Nelessen) that only a *Miss Saigon* can usually afford.

We asked for extra days (in terms of a LORT contract) for technical rehearsal; we asked for extra days for dance rehearsal (there was no one in the show who could not dance and every piece involved movement); Crossroads supported us throughout; even though we knew they thought "plays" didn't require this "showbiz" stuff, they did it with generosity.

Enfin, I believe that Crossroads showed us (me and my collaborators) that a mainstream theatre can sustain us; we showed them technologically wild niggahs ain't so hard to take.

—Ntozake Shange
July 1993

Shelby Jiggetts worked as Literary Manager and Dramaturg at Crossroads Theatre Company in New Brunswick, NJ, and as Associate Dramaturg at Lincoln Center Theater in New York City. She is currently Director of Play Development for The Public Theater/New York Shakespeare Festival.

SELECT BIBLIOGRAPHY

Bridges, Marilyn. *Markings: Aerial Views of Sacred Landscapes.* New York: Aperture, 1986.

Delany, Samuel R. *Stars in My Pocket Like Grains of Sand.* New York: Bantam Books, 1984.

Shange, Ntozake. *for colored girls who've considered suicide/when the rainbow is enuf.* Berkeley: Shameless Hussy Press, 1975; New York: Macmillan Publishing Co., 1977.

———. *The Love Space Demands: A Continuing Saga.* New York: St. Martin's Press, 1992.

CHILDREN OF PARADISE

Shooting a Dream

AT THEATRE DE LA JEUNE LUNE

by Paul Walsh

Theatre de la Jeune Lune, an ensemble company based in Minneapolis, Minnesota, has in its eighteen-year existence become recognized nationally for its imaginative stagings and dynamic, physical style. *Children of Paradise: Shooting a Dream* is based on Marcel Carné's *Les Enfants du Paradis* and the politically charged events surrounding the making of the film in Nazi-occupied France. The company-created epic opened in November 1992, and then toured nationally in 1993, performing at the Yale Repertory Theatre and La Jolla Playhouse. The production was videotaped for the Theatre on Film Archives of the New York Public Library and was awarded the American Theatre Critics Association New Play Award for 1993. The script was subsequently excerpted in *The Best Plays of 1992–1993*, edited by Otis L. Guernsey Jr. and Jeffrey Sweet (New York: Limelight Editions, 1993). Paul Walsh was dramaturg and co-author for this production.

WRITTEN BY	Steven Epp, Felicity Jones, Dominique Serrand, Paul Walsh
BASED ON THE WORK OF	Marcel Carné, Jacques Prévert
DIRECTOR	Dominique Serrand
SCENOGRAPHER	Vincent Gracieux
COMPOSER	Chandler Poling
LIGHTING DESIGNER	Frederic Desbois
COSTUME DESIGNER	Trina Mrnak
DRAMATURG	Paul Walsh

CAST

ARLETTY IN THE ROLE OF GARANCE	Felicity Jones
JEAN-LOUIS BARRAULT IN THE ROLE OF BAPTISTE DEBURAU	Robert Rosen
PIERRE BRASSEUR IN THE ROLE OF FREDERICK LEMAÎTRE	Steven Epp
MARCEL HERRAND IN THE ROLE OF PIERRE-FRANÇOIS LACENAIRE	Charles Schuminski
ROBERT LE VIGAN IN THE ROLE OF JERICHO	John Clark Donahue
MARIA CASARÈS IN THE ROLE OF NATALIE	Sarah Corzatt
MARCEL CARNÉ	Dominique Serrand
JACQUES PRÉVERT	Vincent Gracieux
FRANÇOIS ROSAY	Barbara Berlovitz Desbois
JOSEPH KOSMA	Eric Jensen
ANDRÉ PAULVÉ/STAGE MANAGER OF THE FUNAMBULES	Brian Sostek
ALEXANDRE TRAUNER/ VICHY CENSOR/ PROSECUTOR OF THE PURIFICATION	Michael Collins
MIMI	Laura Esping
DIRECTOR OF PHOTOGRAPHY/PRIEST	Joel Sass
KEY GRIP/GAZELLE	Aimée Jacobson
SOUND ENGINEER	Michael Harryman
FRANÇOIS	Ben Kernan
WARDROBE MISTRESS	Nancy Hogetvedt
MAKEUP ARTIST/AVRIL	Angie Lewis
DIRECTOR OF THE FUNAMBULES/ FRENCH MILITIA/ BBC VOICE JOURNALIST	Terry Ward
CONSTABLE/FRENCH MILITIA/ MME. HERMINE/SET DRESSER	Cherie Anderson
GENERAL HANS SOEHRING/GAFFER	Dave Boerger or Ted Mattison

INTRODUCTION

In Bertolt Brecht's little poem, "Looking for the New and the Old," that inscrutable dramaturg, the Messingkaufer, instructs his actors in the dialectics of cultural production:

> When you read your parts
> Exploring, ready to be surprised,
> Look for the new and the old.

The Messingkaufer's terms are characteristically precise and evocative, as he strives to clarify the complexities of history and social change:

> As the people say, at the moon's change of phases,
> The new moon for one night
> Holds the old in its arms.
> . . . .
> Always fix the "still" and the "already."

The Messingkaufer's "new moon" is both the emblem and the inspiration for the Minneapolis-based Theatre de la Jeune Lune, an ensemble of six theatre artists founded in 1978 by Parisians Dominique Serrand and Vincent Gracieux and Minneapolis natives Barbra Berlovitz Desbois and Robert Rosen. All are graduates of the École Jacques Lecoq in Paris and jointly share the duties of artistic director. Artistic Associate Steven Epp joined Jeune Lune in 1983 and Felicity Jones became an artistic associate in 1985. That same year

Jeune Lune settled permanently in Minneapolis after seven years of splitting its seasons between France and the United States.

The strong and tender care that the future shows for the past at the moon's change of phases describes the dialectic that informs the work of Theatre de la Jeune Lune, linking a past heritage that positions them within the tradition of marginalized vaudevillians, circus performers and commedia entertainers to their present function within their local community and the larger international community of cultural workers. While embracing the "old moon" of theatrical tradition, Jeune Lune seeks to create an entirely new kind of theatre that is highly spirited, physical and visually spectacular. "We are a theatre of directness," the Jeune Lune credo reads, "a theatre that speaks to the audience, that listens and needs its response. We believe that theatre is an event. We are a theatre of emotions—an immediate theatre—a theatre that excites and uses a direct language—a theatre of imagination."

The moon is also the mythical birthplace of the naive innocent Pierrot, a character created by the great pantomime actor Jean-Gaspard Deburau (also frequently spelled Debureau) at the Théâtre des Funambules on the Boulevard du Temple. Pierrot, playing the part of the white-faced dreamer, Baptiste, captured the popular imagination of early nineteenth-century Paris. One night Baptiste fell down from the moon, the story goes, and the white-faced pantomime was born. Since that day the dreamer has longed to return to the moon or capture a bit of its pale magic in his performances. For years, Baptiste's striving after the magic of the moon, especially as immortalized in French film director Marcel Carné's 1945 film *Les Enfants du Paradis*, has inspired and fed the theatrical vision of Theatre de la Jeune Lune. The journey of the dream is their primary scenario; the articulation of half-glimpsed ideas is their goal; the immediacy of performance is their medium. It is natural then that Theatre de la Jeune Lune would turn to *Les Enfants du Paradis* as the source of their largest theatrical production to date.

Early 1989: Genesis of the Idea

It's hard to say exactly where the idea of doing a play based on *Les Enfants du Paradis* began. Steve Epp recalls a conversation sometime in January 1989, in the green room of the Hennepin Center for the Arts in Minneapolis, where the company was performing Kevin Kling's *7 Dwarfs* and rehearsing *1789: The French Revolution*. During this conversation, the idea of dramatizing *Les Enfants du Paradis* was tossed around, though apparently not for the first time. "We had been talking about trying to put *Les Enfants du Paradis* on stage for years," Dominique Serrand remembers. "The film has always been very important to us."

Work on *1789* had turned Dominique's thoughts to the Paris Spring of 1968 and the days he had spent in the Odéon Theatre, which Artistic Director Jean-Louis Barrault had opened to the students of Paris. The classic interior of the Odéon, where the upper balcony is still called "paradis" following seventeenth-century French tradition, served as an inspiring background to the debates of the student revolutionaries over the place that theatre must take in the production of culture. The paradise described in Carné's film—a paradise of audiences and performers creating new realities together out of the power of their collective imagination—suddenly became possible. The presence of Barrault, who had played Baptiste twenty-five years earlier in Carné's film, gave particular significance to the event as past generations spoke to the future.

Over the years, *Les Enfants du Paradis* had remained a per-

The creative team searches for a movie idea: Vincent Gracieux as writer Jacques Prévert; Robert Rosen as actor Jean-Louis Barrault; Dominique Serrand as director Marcel Carné. Photograph by Michal Daniel.

sonal favorite of Dominique and the other members of Theatre de la Jeune Lune. The vision of popular theatre extolled in the film, and the portrait it provides of artists whose passion for art is fed by the passion with which they live their lives, served as a source of inspiration for the company from its earliest days. Here was a statement on art that was as passionate as it was intelligent. Here was a vision of theatre shaping possible futures out of imaginative flights of fancy, of theatre at the center of life, of theatre that works off of life and intervenes on behalf of life but remains always separate from it. Here was a vision of artists transforming reality as they themselves are transformed by it.

Shot during the later years of World War II, when France was occupied in the north by the Nazis and governed in the south by the pro-Nazi government of Vichy, *Les Enfants du Paradis* is a tribute to the power of artists to overcome extraordinary obstacles in pursuit of an idea that from the beginning was both too large and too intricate for the screen. Heralded as the classic culmination of the Golden Age of French filmmaking, Carné's monumental treatment of the politically and emotionally charged nineteenth-century Parisian entertainment district, the Boulevard du Temple (dubbed the Boulevard of Crime for the activities that took place there both onstage and off), has been alternately praised for celebrating the imaginative resiliency of the French and accused of escapist apathy toward their plight. It was Carné's largest collaborative effort and its making was fraught with innumerable difficulties. Shooting began in August 1943, in the Vichy-controlled south of France, only to be interrupted immediately by the Allied invasion of Sicily and the Italian armistice. The film crew was forced to move to Nazi-occupied Paris, where shooting continued under the watchful eye of the Gestapo. It was one of the first films released following the liberation of Paris in 1945. As such, *Les Enfants du Paradis* enjoys mythic stature as a fulcrum of French culture. Though several people involved in making the film, including Carné and his leading lady, Arletty, were later tried for crimes of collaboration by the French Tribunal of the Purification at the end of the war, *Les Enfants du Paradis* remains one of the most loved French films of all time.

I remember a conversation with Dominique one night in February 1989, over a beer in the New French Bar in the Minneapolis warehouse district. *1789* was in rehearsal and Dominique was taking a few minutes to explore a new undertaking. He said the company was thinking about dramatizing *Les Enfants du Paradis*, but as the evening progressed it became clear to me that he was more interested in exploring how films get made. Were there any American films, he asked, surrounded with a mystique, an aura of mystery, a reverence equal to that enjoyed in France by *Les Enfants du Paradis*? Were there any American films that epitomized for American audiences a moment of historical change as succinctly as *Les Enfants du Paradis* did for French audiences? We talked about *The Maltese Falcon*, *Rebel Without a Cause* and *Ben Hur*, about how they filmed the burning of Atlanta in *Gone with the Wind*, and about how Fellini had filmed *The Ship Sails On* in a sound studio on a sea of Mylar. There was something intoxicating in this discussion of how great films are made, something exquisitely theatrical. Transferring a classic film to the stage was a fascinating idea because immediately it raised questions about how things are done, questions that underscore the differences between film and theatre. Dominique asked me to keep the project in mind. It was that evening that my involvement with *Children of Paradise* began.

1789 opened in early March 1989, and the company took off the four days following opening weekend. Steve Epp recalls: "We were all fried to an absolute crisp. I took a few days and went to Chicago. I mean we were absolutely toast that you throw away. Before I left we had been talking about doing *Children of Paradise*, but none of us had a second to think about anything. When I got back, Dominique was talking about doing the making of *Children*

of Paradise. The focus had clearly shifted." That shift—from thinking about putting a film on stage to deciding to do a play about the
making of this particular film—was the most significant decision
in the genesis of this project and it seems to have happened
overnight. "I don't know," Dominique says, "it just seemed more
interesting."

In early May 1989, Steve rented a video of the film and the
company got together to watch it. "I had never seen the film," Steve
admitted later. "The only thing I really knew about it was a reference in Tom Robbins' *Still Life with Woodpecker* about how they
were shooting the film and the Germans came over the hill and
they had to pick up the camera and run. We later found out this
wasn't even true." After viewing the film, the company was generally enthusiastic about the project and a preliminary team was
assembled. Dominique would direct and he invited me to serve as
dramaturg. Steve, Felicity, Dominique and I would compile the scenario and write the script. Vincent would be in charge of the scenography. As with *1789,* directorial and scenographic work would proceed simultaneously with the writing. Dominique asked Frederic
Desbois to design the lights, and Chandler Poling, who had composed the music for *1789,* to write the musical score. With a few
exceptions, notably the substitution of Steve for Barbra and Bob
on the writing team, the project would have nearly the same personnel as had *1789,* and like the earlier epic, this project would be
framed on an historical imperative: a world war, a country occupied, racial genocide and the trials of political purification by
which France tried to redefine or erase its recent history and repo-
sition itself in the modern world. Vincent remembers thinking that
"the idea of doing a movie on stage was exciting from the start, but
the idea of doing this movie—for me as a French person—and
including all the issues surrounding its making, was an idea that was
inspired." Our goal is to be as daring as the work, the people and
the times we are examining.

Memorial Day weekend, 1989

Over the holiday weekend, I borrow a VCR and rent *Les Enfants
du Paradis* to begin puzzling through what this project will be. I
have never seen the film and know relatively little about Carné,
Prévert, Arletty and all the others who will people this play. Despite
the poor quality of the video, the film is astonishing. I watch it half
a dozen times, trying to get a sense of the film and the source of its
greatness. I read the published translation of the film script, sorting
through the intricacies and obscurities of this massive story of love,
jealousy, infidelity and revenge. The more I watch, the more the
characters escape me. Nothing is simple or straightforward about
this elusive story. The dialogue strikes me as quaintly precious, the
environments as foreign and the character motivations as mercur-
ial. The film is slow paced but action packed. Three and a half hours
is too long for a movie and too short to tell this story.

   Members of the company have been reading Edward Baron
Turk's *Child of Paradise: Marcel Carné and the Golden Age of French
Cinema* (Harvard University Press, 1989). I borrow a copy and skim
through it. Turk's Freudian reading of the world of Carné provides
access into the film's trajectory of unfulfilled desires. The structure
of *Les Enfants du Paradis* seems to be governed by the appearance
and disappearance of the central female character, Garance, with
whom each of the four major male characters in the film falls in
love. I sketch out some preliminary notes that discuss the film as a
tale of alienation, frustration and incomprehension; a narrative of
yearning that denies traditional structural expectations to emphasize absence over presence and displacement over fulfillment.
Garance is freedom, adventure and the promise of love. She is the
object of men's desire; but as such, she is always unattainable, and
in the end always absent. Several times the action of the film is suspended for lack of Garance. She is a bird of passage and emblem of
liberty, but she becomes the prize possession of a usurper (the

Count) and is reduced to caged and songless existence. In this, she is like Paris in the 1940s: captive, but free not to sing in the presence of her captor. In the closing shot of the film, Baptiste, the lone individual, stands immobile and speechless at the center of the frame as a rowdy chorus of carnival merrymakers threatens to drown him in a sea of white. Here, as Turk points out, is the existential predicament: the inevitable isolation that accompanies efforts to disengage oneself from the flow of time. The political implications of this are obscure and subverted but intriguing.

July 1989

Since June the writing team has been gathering information on *Les Enfants du Paradis*, on theatre in the 1820s and 1830s and on the situation in France during the occupation. This project will demand massive research. Our clearest idea at the moment is that we will begin our play in the 1820s on the Boulevard of Crime with the watch-stealing scene and pantomime that open the film. This will be staged as a kind of prologue in the lobby using the theatre audience as the crowd on the boulevard. The company experimented successfully with a similar technique in their production of Peter Barnes' *Red Noses* and used it again in *1789,* where a portion of the audience was left standing in the middle of the performance space for the opening scenes of the play. We will bring the audience from the boulevard (in the lobby) to a space representing backstage at the Théâtre des Funambules, where the white-faced pantomime of Baptiste is about to be born, and eventually to their seats as we shift from the fictional world of the 1820s to the political realities of the 1940s.

Several of the key roles have already been tentatively cast. Robert Rosen will play Baptiste and Jean-Louis Barrault. He has the most training in classical pantomime in the company and will

Vincent Gracieux. Photograph by Michal Daniel.

be best prepared to capture and personalize the ephemeral gestures with which Barrault created Baptiste in the film. Felicity Jones will probably play Garance/Arletty. Her uncanny openness and beauty onstage will assist in conveying the mysterious and magnetic power of Arletty and Arletty's characterization of Garance in the film. Steven Epp has the power to carry off the melodramatic gestures of Pierre Brasseur and the great romantic actor Frederick Lemaître without parody or self-conscious commentary. We will keep Charles Schuminski in mind for Marcel Herrand and the poet-assassin Pierre-François Lacenaire; he worked with the company in the 1988 production of *Red Noses* and has enormous power onstage. Similarly, John Clark Donahue, who was in *1789,* would be excellent in any of several roles.

Dominique is not convinced that he should play Carné and direct the show, but the rest of us agree that this is an obvious choice. Since Vincent will be designing the scenography he is the logical one to play Carné's scenic designer, Alexandre Trauner, but we are not sure that we can afford to have Vincent play a character who might end up being relatively minor. Of the company members this leaves only Barbra Berlovitz Desbois. There is no obvious role for Barbra, since we all agree that the role of Natalie and the young actress, Maria Casarès, who played her in the film would not be appropriate for her. Dominique suggests that we construct a character and a role for Barbra from outside the film: a character who blends the qualities of Marlene Dietrich in *The Blue Angel* and the ambiguous eminences in Wim Wenders' *Wings of Desire*, which Dominique and I have recently seen. He calls her Carné's guardian angel and insists that she be both within and outside of historical time. The great actress Françoise Rosay, wife of Carné's mentor, film director Jacques Feyder, and an outspoken advocate for the Free French government in Algiers during the final years of the war, played this role in Carné's life. We need to research this with Barbra in mind.

Beyond that, our ideas about the project and its themes are more general and theoretical. We know that we want to use Carné's film and the story of its creation to examine the struggle of artistic creation under conditions of extreme adversity and to explore the dynamics between art and politics, between artistic collaboration and political acquiescence, and between private visions and social responsibilities. Our goal is neither to vindicate Carné nor to attack him. We are calling our play a study in docu-fiction that takes Carné's film as its primary source. Just as the film constructs a fictional story of desire and displacement out of a web of fact and fantasy, our play will expand outward from the facts and anecdotes about the making of *Les Enfants du Paradis* gleaned from the memoirs of participants and the writings of contemporaries such as Jean-Paul Sartre, Albert Camus, Jean Anouilh, Jean Cocteau, Jean Giraudoux and Jacques Feyder. Our point of origin and primary source will remain the film itself; and like *Les Enfants du Paradis*, our story will blend historical personages and fictional situations. We recognize that we have a responsibility to history as a repository of culture, but we have decided that it is also our responsibility to take liberties with this history, as we had in *1789* and as Carné and Prévert had when making *Les Enfants du Paradis*.

I map out a five-page research prospectus in early July as part of a grant application that we hope will help fund development of the project. In it I outline a demanding schedule for continued exploration:

1) The two distinct cultural-historical periods of the project (Paris in the 1820s through 1830s and France under German occupation) will have to be thoroughly researched, paying particular attention to specific historical chronologies and to the relations between dominant and marginal modes of cultural production particular to each (including issues of censorship and regulation).

2) The film's apparent timidity before trenchant political themes (including the absence of mention of the July Revolution of 1830, though events in the film span the years 1827 to 1833) will have to be more fully explored in terms of the historical events and conditions of its making. In addition, we need to determine the extent to which the historical events of 1943–45, including such things as the arrest of Jews in the French "Free Zone" and the Allied offensive that eventually liberated France, have left traces on the film. This will mean surveying documentary evidence contained in contemporary news sources and materials in the Carné archives (in the French Library in Boston).

3) All the historical personages in the film (especially Jean-Gaspard Deburau, who created the character of Baptiste; the great romantic actor Frederick Lemaître; and the poet-assassin Pierre-François Lacenaire) will have to be carefully researched in an effort to retrace the preliminary steps that Carné and Prévert took in preparing to write the film. In addition, the people involved in the making of the film (Carné, Prévert, Scenographer Alexandre Trauner, Composer Joseph Kosma and each of the major actors) will also have to be studied.

Considerable energy has been spent over the past several months on trying to locate a performance space of a size sufficient to accommodate the proposed project. We will need a space large enough to give the impression of a soundstage and also suggest the scale of historical events that will frame and eventually overwhelm the story of the film. Unfortunately, the Guthrie Theater's warehouse Lab, where *1789* was performed, will not be available in spring 1990, so the company has begun looking at other possible spaces, including the old National Guard Armory downtown.

August 1989

At the end of July 1989, I left Minneapolis for Dallas to take a position teaching theatre history and dramatic literature at Southern Methodist University. Before leaving I assured everyone that I would continue working on *Children of Paradise*, no matter what difficulties this might entail. Now the news from Minneapolis is that the National Guard Armory is tied up in municipal red tape. What now? Dominique has suggested that we consider reducing the scope of the show to fit into the Southern Theater, where Jeune Lune has performed often over the years. This will mean telling the story in miniature with a cast of about ten or so. We could set the play in the farmhouse outside Nice where Trauner and Kosma—both frequent collaborators with Carné on past projects, and both Jewish—were hidden during the months of preparation before filming began. Prévert, Carné, Barrault and other members of the cast show up at the farmhouse to read or act out scenes from the movie as Prévert works on the script, Trauner tinkers with the models of the set; and Kosma plunks away on a piano. The whole play would be a series of clandestine meetings during which the film would take shape. The problem is that this solution would not only squander the scope of *Children of Paradise*, but also infringe upon another idea that Dominique has been talking about for some time: to develop a chamber piece about the creative process and the creation of a myth that would pit Molière and his character Don Juan in debate with Mozart and his Don Giovanni. Rather than allow practical problems to dictate artistic choices, the company decides to continue to search for a suitable venue. The idea of staging preparation work on the film as a series of clandestine meetings, however, remains.

Michael Collins (as set designer Alexandre Trauner) and Vincent Gracieux discuss the film set. Photograph by Michal Daniel.

September 1989

Dominique has come to Dallas for two weeks to work on the scenario, while his application for legal alien status is in the hands of U.S. Immigration. There is no way of determining when a decision will be made or what that decision will be. Perhaps Dominique will have to leave the country. Meanwhile, *Children of Paradise* is still scheduled for spring 1990.

On his first night in Dallas, Dominique unrolls the ground plans for the old St. Paul Train Depot and our project gains a new surge of energy. Here is a venue that will serve our project admirably.

It is vast, textured with history and incredibly versatile. Dominique sketches out various aspects of the building to show how pieces of the emerging scenario will work. Along with discussion of the St. Paul depot comes talk of trains. I hadn't thought about how important trains were throughout the course of the war. Trains were used to transport troops to the front and to transport Jews, Gypsies and other "undesirables" to the Nazi death camps. They were used by those escaping the occupation and by those crossing the frontier from the occupied areas of France in the north to the southern territory governed by the Vichy collaborationists. The train tracks in the St. Paul depot can also double as the tracks on which the film camera rolls for long pans and dolly shots.

As we talk through the scenario and sketch out what we have learned about the months spent planning and writing the film, we begin to realize how much time Carné must have spent traveling between Paris and Provence, where Kosma and Trauner were in hiding and where Victorine Studios were located. What initially we had thought of as meetings in the cafés of Paris to plan the film now become clandestine meetings in train stations and in the farmhouse near Nice. We had noted in earlier discussions how much of the film takes place in marginal settings, transitional enclosures and temporary spaces: backstage, dressing alcoves, staircases, carriages, alleyways, balconies and rental boxes in the theatre. The train station will provide an equivalent from the 1940s to these transitional and temporary spaces. In addition, the dusty, smoky atmosphere of the train station conjures up images from spy movies of the period, giving the sense of an environment fraught with danger and excitement. The scenes depicting the early development of *Les Enfants du Paradis* will replicate the comings and goings of the war itself. (Later we will find the line from Carné's early film *Jenny*— "Life is funny. . . it always has people entering and exiting: arrivals and departures, departures and arrivals"—which will serve as one of several verbal motifs running through our play.)

Our goal during the Dallas sessions has been to come up with a preliminary outline for the show. This has meant focusing on three tasks: 1) talking through the film in detail to identify those parts of the story of *Les Enfants du Paradis* that will be included in our retelling of it; 2) identifying key moments in the making of the film that will help us explore issues of artistic collaboration under adverse conditions; 3) correlating these events from the making of the film with events in the progress of the war. Felicity, Steve and Dominique have done some preliminary work on each of these tasks before Dominique arrived in Dallas. Now we have a three-page sketch of the project that suggests the following five-part structure for *Children of Paradise*:

I. Introduction (in the lobby): theft of the watch; Baptiste's mime.

II. From demobilization of the French army to the beginning of shooting.

   Finding an idea and putting together the production team;

   Trauner and Kosma working clandestinely.

III. Shooting: focus on telling the first part of the story of *Les Enfants du Paradis* from the scenes at the stage door of the Funambules through the Red Breast scenes, the scenes at the boarding house, the introduction of the Count, Lacenaire's crime, and Arletty's arrest and interrogation.

   Insert scenes that show the struggle to make the film under occupation, confrontations with authorities, etc.

   Allied invasion of Sicily and shift of the film crew from Nice to Paris.

IV. Shooting: tell what is crucial from Part II of *Les Enfants du Paradis*.

Shift the focus from the story of the 1830s to the struggle to complete the film and the impact of the war.

Changing political environment with Allied invasion
of Normandy and eventual liberation of Paris.

V. Editing the film amidst accusations of collaboration;
arrests and Trials of the Purification.

Using earlier notes, the printed film script and various visual
documents that we collected over the summer, we begin to ana-
lyze *Les Enfants du Paradis* to see where we might open up space in
that intricate story to tell our story of the film's making. We are
unsure of how much of the story of the film we can tell, or how
much we need to tell. We know we want to focus on those scenes
from the film that make reference, however elusive, to the 1940s.
We decide that for our purposes we will focus primarily on the
events depicted in Part I of the film; from Part II we will include
Lacenaire's murder of the Count and the tangled rekindling of the
stories of love and jealousy provided in the Loggia scenes (the
scenes in which Lemaître visits the Funambules, discovers Garance
and then talks with Baptiste backstage; and the scenes in which
Baptiste, Garance and the Count see Lemaître perform *Othello* at
the Grand Theater and meet backstage, where Lacenaire humili-
ates the Count by drawing aside a curtain to reveal Garance and
Baptiste kissing). We realize that any solution to staging these scenes
will ultimately have to be both scenographic and dramaturgical. As
we study the camera movements and angles used to shoot these
scenes, we discover Carné's fascination with tracing the trajectory
of the gaze of desire from character to character. The camera captures the journey of each character's eyes from the object of desire
to the obstacle that keeps that object always inaccessible. Rather
than trying to differentiate onstage the various locales depicted in
this complicated series of scenes, we decide instead to emphasize

the movement of the gaze of desire as it maps out the emotional and psychological journeys of each of the various characters.

The film's treatment of the theatrical environments and offerings on the Boulevard of Crime will be of special importance to our play, but without the support of the cast of Daumier-like audience members that Carné had at his disposal, it will be difficult to reproduce onstage the effect these scenes have on film. We will have to find another way to capture the magic and pathos of Deburau's *pantomime blanc* if our project is to succeed. Dominique makes some initial sketches of flats representing a theatre audience, and devises an exquisite concept for staging Deburau's famous pantomime of the moon using reflected light in a pool of water in front of the boarding house where Baptiste flees from Garance.

We decide that we want our audience to take the journey of the making of the film without ever really knowing how it turned out, and we agree to avoid imposing closure by never providing a complete understanding of what the film is or says. We want our play to send people out to see the film for the first time or to experience it again in a new way. Our method will be that of Jacques Prévert: "You can't tell the story of a film just like that. It's like an orange, you cannot explain an orange . . . you can peel it, you can eat it, that's all." Though no film is ever shot in sequential order, we decide to trace the story of the film chronologically in the shooting sequences of our play to give the audience a sense of the flow of the complicated love story rather than the discontinuity of actual shooting schedules. Still, it would be valuable to try to locate the shooting log from the film to check where, when and in what order certain scenes were shot.

In trying to isolate the effects of the war and occupation on the making of *Les Enfants du Paradis*, we are struck by the film's apparent hesitancy to acknowledge the crucial political issues of the day. The most important stories linking the filming of *Les Enfants du Paradis* to the occupation and the war are those of Arletty's affair with the German officer Hans Soehring, and the eventual departure from the film and disappearance of Robert Le Vigan, the actor who played Jericho in the early days of shooting and an anti-Semitic supporter of the Nazis. Le Vigan was replaced in the role of Jericho by Pierre Renoir. It will be our task over the coming months to determine what other effects the occupation and war had on the making of the film.

The script would have had to be passed by the Vichy censors and ultimately approved by the German occupiers. Considering the subject matter of the film, this would have been more difficult than it would at first appear, since at the time the Vichy authorities adhered to a program of "moral reform" and "family values" that not only prohibited the treatment of adultery and extramarital sex but also was sensitive to all hints of political allegory. Carné and Prévert had already come under attack for their earlier film, *Les Visiteurs du Soir,* and Carné had been vilified in the press as a Jewish sympathizer and sexual deviant.

Might the film's political timidity be more apparent than real? Despite their differences, both Carné and Prévert located themselves on the margins of French cultural production, though each had his own idea of what the mainstream was. Prévert was the outspoken ringleader of the surrealist Group Octobre, a clandestine member of the Resistance and a public figure of dissidence. Carné was more old fashioned in many ways—he refused the fashions of modernism for example—but he was more subversive than most of his contemporaries when it came to issues of social morality; and under the directives on public morality issuing from Vichy, this proved politically problematical for Carné.

The whole issue of censorship and self-censorship is very much in our minds these days as the National Endowment for the Arts comes under attack and the religious right in America is demanding support for what they euphemistically call "family values." We are struck, moreover, by the similarities between the contemporary rhetoric of censorship and the statements and restrictions issued by Vichy in support of Pétain's program of moral reforms. Dominique suggests a line of dialogue that intimates the retreat of politics into the obscurantism of allegory: "Why do you use an accordion player when it is clear you want a violin?" Kosma asks Carné. "Because when I see the pounding, I hear the boots of the storm troopers." (Our play will ultimately have both violin and accordion, though not these lines.)

October 1989–August 1990

With a loose three-page outline finally in place and a potentially suitable space under negotiation, the project seems possible again. Dominique has finally received his green card from U.S. Immigration, but now a new panic sets in as we begin to realize how much work needs to be done in the next three months to start rehearsals as planned in early 1990. I have arranged to go to Minneapolis as soon as the fall term ends in early December and stay until classes begin again in January. Over the next few weeks, however, negotiations with the city of St. Paul for use of the train depot break down and *Children of Paradise* is again postponed, this time indefinitely.

The decision to postpone *Children of Paradise* is both difficult and exhilarating. Above all, it underscores the company's commitment to producing the work on the scale originally envisioned for the project. No one doubts that *Children of Paradise* will happen. When, how and where are now the issues, and what shape the project will take when it finally does come together. The decision to postpone is also a decision on the part of the company to focus their efforts on securing a permanent home.

In August 1990, Theatre de la Jeune Lune announces a $2.85 million capital campaign to purchase and renovate the old Allied Van Lines cold storage building in the Minneapolis "warehouse

Filming the dressing room sequence. Photograph by Michal Daniel.

district." Working closely with the architectural firm of Arvid Elness and principal architect Paul Madson, they plan the "creative demolition" of the interior of the warehouse. The proposal is to carve offices and a flexible 6,000-square-foot performance space out of the block-long five-story building without damaging the red-brick Gothic facade added to the building in 1906 by architect Cass Gilbert and protected by the National Register of Historic Places.

October 1991–March 1992

After an extraordinarily successful capital campaign, the company purchases the building on December 7, 1991. Renovations will begin in April. We now know where and when *Children of Paradise* will be performed. Our epic exploration of art and artists will open the new building in the fall of 1992. New schedules have been drawn up and research is beginning again in earnest. At the end of October 1991, I visited Minneapolis with a pile of research documents, several of the published film scripts of various Carné-Prévert collaborations, and a couple hundred pages of photocopies on French cultural politics and filmmaking in the 1940s, on the Boulevard of Crime and on various of the personalities we are interested in exploring. There is a small meeting room in the company's offices in the Berman Buckskin Building with a window that looks across the street to Jeune Lune's future home. It is in this room that we will spend the spring and summer of 1992 constructing *Children of Paradise*. Following the process we had used to compile and write *1789*, we will cover the walls with poster board and sketch the scenario out in storyboard fashion, decorating the walls graffiti-style with notes, quips, drawings and clippings that reveal the skeletal shape and internal growth of our story.

In the meantime, the shelves in the meeting room have become the repository for research materials: books, notes, newspaper clippings, photographs and other miscellaneous materials gathered over the intervening years as the project has matured and grown. I have been meeting with Steve Epp on my various trips to Minneapolis since the fall of 1989, to keep abreast of how and where the research for the project has been going. Members of the writing team have been reading widely in the memoirs and biographies of the various people from the 1820s and the 1940s whom we are interested in treating. Sometimes leads have pointed in unexpected directions, as when we learned that Maria Casarès, who played Natalie in the film, was the protégée of Marcel Herrand, who played Lacenaire, and that this was her first film. When Steve is struck by the importance Barrault gave to the poet Robert Desnos in his memoirs, Vincent brings in copies of some of his poems and provides impromptu translations and background on this tragic victim of the Nazi death camps. "Desnos has always been one of my favorite poets," Vincent says, "and his tragic story as a member of the Resistance who was deported and died two days after the Americans liberated the death camp in Czechoslovakia haunted me since I was thirteen or fourteen years old. I knew Prévert first of course because growing up in France in those days, when you were fourteen you read Prévert. But from Prévert, I went on to Desnos. They've been with me for many years." Notes, incidents, anecdotes, philosophical asides and characterizing observations are noted on scraps of paper, written into personal notebooks or filed in memory to be dug out during the writing sessions in the summer of 1992. In the meantime the company continues the daily routine of running a theatre, mounting a season of plays that meets with unprecedented success and steering the capital campaign that will finance its new home.

As plans are finalized for the renovation of the warehouse, we begin to see the scenography and the shape of our play coming to life. The architectural model of the building provides an exhilarating point of focus when discussing the evolving scenario. More is suddenly possible in this new space than could have been imagined previously. The projected lobby seems to have been designed specifically for the opening sequence of the play on the Boulevard of Crime; and the red-brick interior walls of the playing space conjure up a past history rich with theatrical possibilities. When we return to work on *Children of Paradise* in earnest in April 1992, much has already been achieved.

April 1992

Dominique returns to Dallas for ten days in early April 1992, to see where we are and where we need to be to begin compiling the

script as soon as I can get to Minneapolis in late May. One thing
that constantly amazes me about working with Jeune Lune is their
ability to remember. When Dominique and I set to work again on
Children of Paradise, all of the previous conversations are still in
place, complicated now and enhanced by the ongoing research and
changing perspectives of the intervening years. The memoirs of
the artists involved in the film have added new depth and detail to
our conception. As our attention shifts from the film to the community of artists who came together to make it, we are more convinced than ever that this is a story worth telling. Ours will be a
story of personal passions and preoccupations that will treat not
only the need for and purpose of art in the contemporary world,
but also the innumerable difficulties that beset it. While new sets of
questions arise, however, the basic frame, outlined in fall 1989,
remains intact.

As Dominique and I are meeting in Dallas, Steve and Felicity
continue their work in Minneapolis, communicating with us by
phone and fax. A quotation from Carné heads one such transmis-
sion of questions, suggestions and fragmentary ideas: "Most of the
time we succeeded in composing (scenes) only after one of us had
yielded to the other. Our working principle was to spurt out what-
ever came into our heads." (In the coming months we will learn
how fruitful this method can be.) In Dallas, Dominique and I are
watching dozens of movies, movies of all kinds: movies by the great
auteurs like Truffaut, Renoir, Fellini and Antonioni, as well as
Hollywood thrillers like *Terminator* and *Wild Orchid*. Sometimes we
talk about what we are watching and sometimes Dominique simply mutters something about "that shot" or "the lighting there" and
I try to figure out what's catching his attention. We decide that we
must begin thinking of the writing as if we were composing a
movie: constructing each moment of our story as if it were a film
shot and paying particular attention to how each moment is framed
in time and space. This will demand constant attention to the pres-

ence or absence of the camera onstage, the direction it is facing and the segment of the theatrical scene it is framing. Lighting instruments, sound boom and film crew will each play a vital role in framing, commenting on and shaping moments of a much larger theatrical experience. We are fascinated by the elliptical quality of film writing and decide to try to capture this onstage. We will construct our scenario as a kind of thriller, with scenes and speeches intimating a deeper significance that will never be confirmed.

When I bring up the tricky Loggia scenes that had stymied us in earlier meetings, Dominique simply says, "I think Vincent and I have solved that." Vincent recalls that when he and Dominique had sat down to review the scenography before Dominique came to Dallas, they were already talking in terms of camera moves. The various set pieces of the Red Breast and Loggia scenes would be designed to open up so that the camera could move in and out in front of and behind the action, providing the impression of multiple points of perspective. "Dominique had the whole travel of the camera in his mind," Vincent recalls. "It was sometimes difficult to follow exactly what he was saying, but he had a very precise idea of it all in his mind—of what planes [of the set] should be seen, of what the point of view of the actors toward the camera would be at each moment, of how parts of one scene would move away to become the background for the next shot. All of that." Before coming to Dallas, Dominique had contacted the Film in the Cities museum in Minneapolis and learned that they had a couple of period cameras on dollies, including a crane dolly; he is building the show with these in mind.

Marketing Director Steve Richardson is clamoring for a title for the show so the 1992–93 season can be announced. Various titles, serious and otherwise, are suggested (*Children of Paradise: Shot During World War II, They Shoot Children of Paradise, Don't They?, Shooting the Mime*) before we finally settle on *Children of Paradise: Shooting a Dream*, which we feel suggests the ambiguity and cap-

The movie crew filming Charles Schuminski (as Marcel Herrand/Pierre-François Lacenaire) and Felicity Jones (as Arletty/Garance). Photograph by Michal Daniel.

tures the richness of our project. Respect for an audience that is poor and hungry but worthy of artistic nourishment was a theme dear to Jacques Prévert. For us, however, the title *Children of Paradise* refers not only to the poorer sections of the audience in the upper balcony of the Funambules, or to the actors who performed for them. It also conjures up contrasting images of the children who were victimized by the war and especially those who died in the Nazi death camps. At the same time, the title calls to mind the Hitler youth who were the children who would people the paradise of the Third Reich.

Steve and Felicity have given considerable attention to Part II of the September 1989 outline, underscoring the importance of a slow delineation of the connections between the actors in the 1940s before linking them to the characters they played in the film. They suggest that we move from the scenes at the Funambules to a meeting or series of meetings between Carné, Prévert and Barrault at a café in the south of France for the section of the original outline that dealt with events "from the demobilization of the French army to the beginning of shooting." Carné and Prévert would discuss the recent attacks on Carné as a "slave of the Jews" in the right-wing press. Barrault would enter with stories of life at the Comédie-Française and of his romance with Madeleine Renaud. Each would tell stories of the Phony War (September 1939–March 1940, just after the collapse of Poland; a period of relative military inaction on the Franco-German front, derided by journalists), and demonstrate differences in character according to their different attitudes toward the war: the romantic (Barrault), the cynic (Prévert), and the impotent (Carné). Eventually Barrault would bring up the idea of a movie based on the life and trial of Jean-Gaspard Deburau. (All of this would later be condensed into the scene called "Provence.")

A later fax suggests adding two more scenes or segments to the early meetings in which the idea for *Les Enfants du Paradis* was finally fixed: a scene between Carné and Paulvé, and a scene between Carné and Rosay (later condensed into the Train Station scenes in the final scenario). In the first, Carné and Paulvé would discuss being artists in France and debate the contradictions and dangers of film production under the occupation. They would also discuss the scam devised by the German-controlled Continental Pictures, which oversaw film production in occupied France, to entice the big names of the French cinema to work for them. Paulvé would declare his intention to make another movie with Carné and Prévert after the success of *Les Visiteurs du Soir*, but also express his concern that as an independent producer he had enemies among the upper echelons of Continental. In order to get a license, the new movie would have to deal with a safe and popular topic that would not offend the authorities. In the next scene Madame Rosay would bring news about who was doing what among the French artistic émigrés in America and raise questions about whether one should leave France or stay. How far do events have to progress before they directly affect us, our decisions and our work?

As these notes arrive from Minneapolis, Dominique and I continue to talk through bits of the scenario and aspects of character, reacquainting ourselves with where we have been and where we are going. The political equivocation of Carné's film continues to both trouble and excite us, as does what Jacques Bazin calls its "elliptical elegance." We realize that we will not be able to visit the Carné archives in Boston since there is no time when both Dominique and I would be available for such a trip and there is no money in the budget for research. Earlier in the year I had spoken by telephone with the curator of the collection and learned that much of it was as yet uncatalogued, that certain papers were closed to the public, and that a lot of the collection was packed away in trunks. Without access to personal correspondences, the political equivocation of the film noted early in the project will be difficult to trace or substantiate. Instead we decide to focus on the complexities implicit in Carné's statement that he just wanted to make movies. We will hold to our goal of seeking neither to vindicate nor to vilify Carné, but we are aware that the very act of making this play and celebrating this film is far from neutral.

Dominique is looking for ways of keeping Carné from becoming the center of our play. He is also concerned about the role of Françoise Rosay. Barbra has been reading the memoirs of Feyder and Rosay and sends us several pages of suggestions, quotations and observations that give new substance to this elusive role. Rosay becomes the voice of the Free French government in Algiers speaking on the radio to the German women; she will also serve as a central figure in the Trials of the Purification that will close our play.

Dominique leaves Dallas in late April with promises that the writing team will have a first draft of the scenario ready for our first scheduled writing meeting in Minneapolis on June 1.

June 1992

Exactly three years after I first watched *Les Enfants du Paradis*, I join Steve, Felicity, Dominique and Vincent in the Jeune Lune offices in Minneapolis to hear where we stand and begin the next leg of the project. Our goal is to finalize the scenario and to produce a first draft of the play by July 8. As daunting as this task seems, we are all more or less confident in the work we have done over the past several years and feel that, however unrealistic this goal might seem, we will do our best to achieve it. We listen for two days as Steve talks through the scenario in detail, with assistance and interruptions from the rest of us. Questions are raised, difficulties clarified and alternatives articulated in a free flow of ideas. Whenever anything isn't clear to any of us, we ask for clarification. Sometimes clarifications follow, sometimes not. Whenever we are uncomfortable about making specific decisions on issues that we have not explored fully yet, we make a note of alternatives. Throughout the two days I jot down copious notes which, after another week of detailed discussion, I begin to translate into a fifteen-page document that presents the scenario in seventeen scenes or groups of scenes:

AcT I

1. Boulevard of Crime (Prologue and Backstage at the Funambules)
2. Train Station Scenes
3. Provence
4. Design Meeting
5. Shooting (The Red Breast Scenes)
6. Invasion of Sicily
7. Shooting in Paris (The Dressing Room Scenes)
8. Reverie (The Drive South)
9. Arrests

Intermission

AcT II

10. Murder of Carné
11. The Loggia Scenes
12. Air Raid
13. Purgatory
14. Liberation of Paris
15. Projection Room
16. Trials of the Purification
17. Epilogue

The scenario provides a detailed account of the action and themes of each scene as well as notes on music, atmosphere, tone, character development and scenographic details. Strategies for making transitions from one scene to the next are noted and details about character motivations and thematic ambiguities are included as appropriate. The scenario will serve as our guide in the upcoming months in compiling and composing the script. It will also serve as a summary of the project for Composer Chandler Poling, Lighting Designer Frederic Desbois, and Scenographer Vincent Gracieux until the script is completed.

It soon becomes evident as we work to finalize the scenario with the model of the new building in front of us that it will not be practical to move the audience from the boulevard to backstage at the Funambules and then to their seats. Not only would this necessitate constructing a whole backstage life that would be difficult with the limited number of actors at our disposal, but it would also create logistical nightmares for the scenographer and probably take more time than it would be worth. We decide instead to incorporate what is crucial from the scenes backstage at the Funambules into the prologue itself (called "Boulevard of Crime" in the scenario) and move directly into the theatre from the lobby. Here, as elsewhere, we discover that many of the scenes we thought were vital to our retelling of the story of the movie can be condensed in the scenario and more deliberately interspersed with scenes and incidents from the 1940s. We rededicate ourselves to following Carné's lead. Just as Carné treated theatrical fiction in his film as a series of truncated and elliptical snippets that remain always unsatisfying, so we will treat the moments selected from the film as inconclusive fragments that intimate more than they reveal.

We also discover early on that if we are going to bring the show in at under twelve hours, we will have to sacrifice some ideas that we have grown attached to, including Steve and Felicity's suggestion of an elaborate series of scenes depicting the planning of the film, with Carné traveling by train between Paris (Villancourt Studios), Nice (Victorine Studios and the country farmhouse where Trauner and Kosma were in hiding) and "La Prieure" in Provence where Prévert was staying. Instead, the Design Meeting

(Scene 4) will take place in a single locale—blending Prévert's "Little Heaven" in Provence and the farmhouse near Nice where Trauner and Kosma were hiding—visited by Carné, Barrault, Brasseur, Paulvé, Herrand and Casarès. Carné's insistence on maintaining the integrity of his movie ("If you don't want to do this film, I will do something else; but I will not change my movie") becomes less important thematically than the excitement of getting started. Our early discussions of the play would have brought contemporaries such as Jean-Paul Sartre, Jean Anouilh, Louis Jouvet and Jean Giraudoux onto the stage, but these personages now prove tangential to our story. The existentialism of Sartre and of Camus (with whom Maria Casarès was having an affair at the time) will instead be filtered through Prévert and Herrand. Similarly, the intrigues and anecdotes surrounding Barrault acting and directing at the Comédie-Française during the filming will have to be reduced, though Barrault's theatrical dreams and his life-long devotion to Madeleine Renaud will remain central to the journey of that character.

One of the first things that struck us when we began researching the making of *Les Enfants du Paradis* was the ironic tragedy that befell Trauner's set of the boulevard, constructed on the lot of Victorine Studios at a cost greater than any previous set in the history of French filmmaking. Three days after shooting began, the Allied forces landed in Sicily. The film crew was ordered to abandon the set and return to Paris. When Carné returned to Nice several months later, the set had been destroyed in a storm. We have tried to work out a way of showing Trauner's destroyed set onstage at the end of the section called "Reverie" (Scene 8), but are ultimately forced to acknowledge the theatrical impossibility of this fundamentally cinematic scene. Our compromise of including this in the dialogue is a pale ghost of our earliest conception, but at times it is imperative to accept the limitations of our medium and move on.

Steven Epp as actor Pierre Brasseur performing the film role of Frederick Lemaître; and Felicity Jones as the actress Arletty performing the film role of Garance. Photograph by Michal Daniel.

We had talked a good deal in the early days of reproducing on our stage the fanciful dramaturgy of the nineteenth-century Theater of Spectacle, and we researched some of the extant scripts from the Théâtre des Funambules. We realize now that we won't be able to stage an actual nineteenth-century pantomime, and focus instead on Baptiste's pantomime of the moon, which will serve as a transition from the scenes in the boarding house at the end of the Red Breast segment (Scene 5) to the Allied invasion of Sicily (Scene 6). Dominique explains his idea for showing the reflected moon first on the window of Garance's room in the boarding house and then in a pool of water in front of the boarding house where it is discovered by Baptiste. He admits, however, that this might be too complicated to carry off. In any case, we hope the pantomime of the moon will capture some of the sense of nostalgia and regret at the heart of Carné's movie, and provide a theatrical parallel to Carné's veneration of the cinematic heritage of the silent-film era.

The scenario digresses at several significant points from the September 1989 outline, and at times from what we know about the actual shooting of the film. Sections II and III of the 1989 outline have been greatly reduced from what we had originally planned. The Allied invasion of Sicily and the shift from Nice to Paris come much earlier. We also decide that by separating the abandoning of Trauner's set in Nice and the departure of producer André Paulvé from the film after he was "declared Jewish" by the Vichy authorities (now in the scene called "Purgatory"), we can heighten the drama of these two events. We sacrifice mention of the German ban on Franco-Italian coproductions (including *Les Enfants du Paradis*) following the Italian armistice, and the outcry of Parisian journalists attempting to save the project, because this will demand too much exposition. We decide instead to focus on stories of crew members on the film being hunted by the Gestapo, and begin to explore the implications of Carné's mention in his memoirs that the production manager on the film was a leader in the Resistance.

In a difficult passage in his memoirs, Carné had recounted how a crew member on the shoot was lured away from the set and arrested one day with a story about his wife having been seriously injured. When the production manager was asked how he could have let this happen, he said "they spoke French." As a leader in the Resistance, he should have known better. In any case this would serve as an excellent parallel to the arrest of Garance at the end of Part I of the film. Garance produces the Count of Monterey's card and is released. In the 1940s, as in the 1820s, "misfortune does not always choose which door it knocks on." Unfortunately Carné has no calling card that will buy his release from the realities of this world at war. Carné's staging of Garance's release becomes a deliberate fictional rewriting of a political reality that had become too present in the making of the film. In our play the Resistance leader/production manager becomes Mimi, script girl on the shoot and Carné's assistant. Mimi soon becomes a particular favorite of ours and the occasion for endless banter and jokes that never make their way into the script. It is unfortunate that Mimi will never be fully developed as a character, but she will be shown interrogating a former member of the Gestapo following the liberation of Paris, in a scene inspired by a passage in Marguerite Duras' *The Wars*; and she will be an important presence in the Trials of Purification.

There are several contradictory reports of when the actor Robert Le Vigan left the film. Carné insisted that Le Vigan was replaced early in the role of Jericho by Pierre Renoir, but other reports suggest that nearly half the Jericho scenes had to be reshot. Le Vigan is reported to have left Paris for Denmark with Céline shortly after D-Day. In any case, we decide that for the sake of our play we will keep Le Vigan around as long as possible and, like Jericho in the film, he will appear as if from the middle of nowhere.

As soon as the initial scenario is completed we go back to the beginning and write a second working scenario in which we attempt to map out each scene in moment-by-moment detail. This helps to clarify the overall flow of the play and to identify transitional points where things remain elusive. At the same time we begin translating, editing and assembling those scenes from the film script that we will use for the boulevard and shooting scenes (Scenes 1, 5, 7, 9, 11, 13 and 15). Moments from the film that may prove useful elsewhere are transcribed and pasted onto the storyboards that cover the walls of the meeting room. In the corner of the room is a table piled with a constantly changing array of books and papers that people thumb through at various moments during the writing sessions in search of inspiration, half-remembered ideas or sources of language. We strive to capture in our dialogue the witty tone and surrealist sensibility of Prévert, the anxiety and introspection of Sartre, the pace of the Hollywood movies of the

1940s and the mood of the films of the Golden Age of French cinema. The task is immense, but we know we can also rely on a performance style and scenography that will enhance and underscore the desired effect.

There is a real advantage in writing for a company of actors whose abilities and strengths one knows intimately. There is even greater advantage in having those same actors write for themselves. Steve takes charge of the role of Frederick Lemaître and constructs the great Romantic actor to take advantage of his own strengths as an actor. He also takes responsibility for researching Pierre Brasseur, who played Lemaître in the movie, and finds an amazing array of correspondences between the two. It is fascinating to watch an actor's research blend with and feed the construction of the character he will play, rather than proceed after the fact. Similarly, Felicity is a passionate defender of the intricacies of Garance's situation as presented in the film, and reminds us of our early decision to give the audience enough of the film to allow them to care for these characters and their predicaments before shifting to and blending this story with that of the 1940s.

I am convinced that this is a three-act show with a first intermission following the Invasion of Sicily (Scene 6). This will give us more time to pursue the planning and development of the movie, but it will also make for a much longer show. Dominique convinces me that two intermissions are death and I agree to set my reservations aside. Steve has been thinking about a transition into Act II that will catch the audience by surprise and restate the suspense structure intimated in Act I. He suggests opening the act with an ambiguous scene in which someone apparently murders Carné, but it is later revealed as a rehearsal of the filming of the murder of the Count. No one is really convinced that this is the right solution, though there is something intriguing about it. (Eventually we decide to open the act with Baptiste's murder of a man in the street [Jericho] that had been part of the initial inspiration for the film, and then reveal this as Prévert's unsuccessful attempt to convince Carné of the ending he has envisioned for the story.) Several such loose ends remain in the scenario despite our best efforts to resolve as many difficulties and answer as many questions as possible.

Vincent is busy designing a model of the boulevard and of the set pieces for the Red Breast, Dressing Room and Loggia scenes. He spent a Saturday afternoon recently watching the movie with his finger on the pause button, stopping each time a piece of set could be seen in the frame. He was trying to determine how many different set pieces were used in each segment of the film. He has also compared stills of Trauner's set of the boulevard to actual engravings of the boulevard from the 1820s and 1830s to get a sense of how Trauner interpreted his subject. Just as Trauner enhanced some buildings and diminished others in his reconstruction of the boulevard, so Vincent is altering the size and dimensions of the Funambules to give it more prominence in his model of the "street of many murders." The challenge of this set, Vincent will admit later, was to create "as many options for different points of view as possible. I was very interested in how shots were being framed and I found inspiration in the paintings of Balthus. The color, the design and sense of frame, and the interplay of light and shadow in Balthus were very important to me in designing this set because they are so cinematic."

Since September 1989, Dominique has said that he wants a moving train in the play. Vincent has sketched out plans for a train that stretches the whole length of the lobby and will be visible through the doors and windows in the wall that separates the lobby from the playing space. In one sketch, there is an engineer who looks like Jean Gabon, with a cigarette dangling from his lips. We add the character to our personnel list, knowing full well that we already have more characters onstage than we will be able to accommodate. Dominique and Steve have already cornered Michael Harryman, Jeune Lune's box office manager, and persuaded him to

Felicity Jones and Robert Rosen in the street scene prologue. Photograph by Michal Daniel.

take the nonspeaking role of the sound engineer, Gilles Martin, in Act I. Since Gilles doesn't appear onstage until Scene 5 and is arrested by the Gestapo at the end of Act I, Michael will have time to close up the box office and attend to all his other duties besides. Early on, Dominique had said that he wanted to have children playing in the train station when the audience moved into the theatre from the lobby. One of the boys would hold a comb against his upper lip to become Hitler and scare the girls. This idea has since had to be abandoned.

Dominique has contacted Trina Mrnak about designing costumes for the show. She needs a fairly accurate count of characters and costumes sometime in the next week so she can decide whether the show can be costumed within the allotted budget. Using the scenario as our guide, we begin to think through the project in terms of personnel and come up with a scene-by-scene breakdown of which characters are involved in which scenes and who is available to double in minor roles. We talk through the thematic implications of costume changes, discussing, for example, when the characters will be in costumes from the 1940s and when they will be dressed as the characters they are playing from the 1820s.

The next step is to confirm the casting of the show and contract actors from outside the company. We have been thinking for some time that we could not afford to have Vincent play the minor role of Trauner. Looking at the scenario, we realize how minor this role has become and ask Vincent to play the screenwriter Jacques Prévert. In deciding that Vincent will play Prévert, we also commit Prévert to a central place in our scenario and begin making adjustments to have him appear in various scenes where he had not previously been present. Vincent is of course thrilled to be asked to play Prévert, one of his boyhood heroes, and he has begun to feed us anecdotes and observations about the role from some of Prévert's autobiographical writings (particularly *Choses et Autres* and *Hebdromadaires*).

Dominique has contacted Charles Schuminski about taking the part of Herrand/Lacenaire and he has asked John Clark Donahue to play Le Vigan/Jericho. Sarah Corzatt, who performed with the company in its spring 1992 show, *The Ballroom*, is cast as Maria Casarès/Natalie and will play violin and accordion as needed. In early June, Dominique ran into Eric Jensen, who performed Chan Poling's music in *1789,* and asked him if he would be interested in playing for *Children of Paradise* and taking the minor role of Joseph Kosma. Later Eric would admit: "I had no idea what this show would be, but I had been around in 1989 when they first started talking about *Children of Paradise*, and I'd seen the film and other work by the 'frogs' [Jeune Lune], and I knew Chan's music and I thought, well okay, we'll see what this will be." Joel Sass, who has worked on several recent Jeune Lune shows, has agreed to serve as the show's production manager and head the film crew onstage as

"Director of Photography." Once the key roles and positions are cast, Dominique will think at more leisure about hiring additional actors and extras to play Paulvé, Trauner, Mimi, the censor and a dozen or so other minor roles.

Dominique and I meet with Fred Desbois to talk through the scenario and discuss the lighting. I am surprised at how much sense the scenario makes as we talk through it and how clear it all sounds. Dominique insists that the lighting be cinematic and on an operatic scale. They discuss the filtered gray light in the train stations of Paris at some length and Dominique says he is very interested in using onstage instruments and reflected light throughout the play. Film in the Cities has a couple vintage lighting instruments that they will lend us and we will construct other effects—like the rain effect for the end of the Red Breast scenes (Scene 5)—as necessary. Fred is particularly concerned that we find a lightboard operator who will be able to handle the musical subtleties of the lighting design he will create.

By mid-June the company has finalized negotiations to take *Children of Paradise* to the Yale Repertory Theatre in January 1993. It is planned that Yale School of Drama students will have an opportunity to meet the Jeune Lune company and perhaps take part in the production while we are in residency in New Haven. We have known for a long time that this would be an important project for the company but, as Steve remembers, "we had no idea how big it was. Once we got into it, it was bottomless." We decide to avoid this thought now, and convince ourselves that this is just another show. We need to limit our thoughts to opening night.

"Vacation was approaching," Steve recalls, "and we were all feeling really good about the scenario. It was detailed, flushed out, incredibly dense and rich and, most surprising of all, it was in sync with what we'd been saying and thinking about from the start." We divide up the early scenes of the scenario and each of the four writers comes in with sketches of various scenes and reads them to the others. Then everyone else suggests changes, new lines and rewrites. There is a great sense of collective ownership and very little ego. In this way we work through or rough out much of Act I, with the exception of Scene 4 (Design Meeting) and Scene 8 (Reverie). Unfortunately, we are still working on the "twelve-hour version" of the script. ("It will take the time it takes," Carné said in one version of the script. The line was eventually cut for time as we worked in fall 1992 to bring *Children of Paradise* in at under four hours. I still miss it.)

We take two days to talk in detail through the individual journeys of each of the major characters of the 1940s to insure that we have included each crucial step in each individual story at the appropriate place in the scenario. This proves a very valuable exercise because it alerts us to the multiple stories we are telling and forces us to confirm from a new position of understanding many of the choices we had made intuitively over the years. It is during these discussions that we decide definitely not to show the Count onstage and to reduce the role of Hans Soehring, the Nazi officer with whom Arletty had an affair, to a few haunting visual images. Both decisions are more than simply pragmatic. Each continues and confirms our analysis of the film in terms of absences and fragments. We are intrigued by the idea of referring to both a fictional world and an historical reality that can never be fully reproduced or represented onstage. The same is true of our introduction into the script of Robert Desnos (whom some would later say was one of the most important characters of the play, though he never appeared onstage), and of the whole issue of the deportation and incarceration of the Jews. Just as the Count will be manifested in other people (Carné, Rosay, Prévert), so the horrors of the war will find concrete and specific points of intrusion through the details of the lives of our characters.

July–August 1992

We have not gotten as far as we had hoped with the writing, but we are still optimistic about the project. We spend the first week of July talking through those scenes in the scenario that are still vague, particularly the second half of Act II, from the Air Raid through Purgatory and the Liberation of Paris. We decide at this point that the Liberation and Trials will blend into each other while Carné is consumed with the final editing of his film (the Projection Room scene).

In sketching out the scenario, we had planned that the trials would include an interrogation of the film itself and we talked about putting Carné on trial through various of his characters. Now we focus on the trial of Lacenaire for the murder of the Count. This was not treated in the film, but our analysis of Lacenaire as an existential antihero who embraces the consequences of his actions, and demands recognition from the society he despises, suggested enticing parallels to Prévert, Carné and their collaborative efforts. After discussing the extent to which historical events like the liberation of Paris live on and have become part of history through still photographs and documentary-film footage, we construct a series of visual images for the Liberation scene that will include bicycles, flags and tanks. If we had produced *Children of Paradise* in the National Guard Armory we might in fact have been able to think about using tanks, but somehow I'm not convinced that the miniature remote-control tanks used years ago in the company's production of *Ubu for President* won't trivialize this moment.

People will return from vacation in early August and we will still have nearly a month to work on the script before rehearsals begin in early September. I remind Dominique that we are much further along at this point than we were with *1789* when rehearsals began, but I too am nervous about how much there is to finish.

Still, we do have four months before we open and four months is a long time. We're counting on the fact that people will return from vacation with renewed energy and focus.

Dominique will be home in Paris until early August. I've accepted his invitation to go along for ten days to continue the work in a relaxed and inspiring environment. What I did not anticipate was how omnipresent the spirit of our play would be on the streets of Paris. On the fiftieth anniversary of Operation Spring Breeze (the code name used for the mass arrest of Parisian Jews and their deportation to the camps), the press is filled with stories about the occupation, about Pétain and Vichy, and about the effects of the war on French culture. Everywhere we are reminded of the importance of the subject that has consumed us for the past several months. We visit what is left of the district of the Boulevard du Temple, drive by the buildings Carné used in *Le Jour se Leve* and *Hôtel du Nord*, and look at the nineteenth-century paintings in the Musée d'Orsay. Occasionally we talk specifically about a moment in the scenario, a detail of character, a scenic image or thematic concurrence. Whether in silence or in conversation, when looking or walking or sitting, wherever we are, we are both at work on *Children of Paradise*. My days in France go quickly, and before the end of July I am back in Dallas, preparing for another year of teaching.

After I leave, Dominique takes a train south from Paris with a Super-8 camera and shoots a loop of film from the train window to use in the scene alternately called Reverie or The Drive South (Scene 8). This scene troubled us when we were working on the scenario and I avoided discussing it with Dominique when we were in Paris because I was still not sure how it works or should work. I've learned that sometimes it is best to take on faith those things that are brewing in Dominique's mind and not push prematurely for explanations or clarifications that might obliterate a thought that is still being formulated. In any case, we originally discussed the scene as an extended surreal transition from the Dressing

Room scenes on the Paris soundstage to the destroyed set of the boulevard near Nice. It is the point in the play where the difficulties of the war become realities, and Carné is tempted by Madame Rosay to abandon his film and join the French émigrés in Hollywood or follow her to Algiers to support de Gaulle's government in exile.

The Carné/Rosay meeting was to be a meditative respite in the shooting, but one fraught with conflicting impulses. Carné has faced the difficulties and terrible sense of abandonment that surrounds work on this film when Madame Rosay arrives with stories of Hollywood. The scene shifts in tone to that of the Hollywood movies of the 1940s as they travel southward into a dream. We had talked about those scenes in the movies of the period where riding in a roadster evoked a feeling of release and freedom, and we toyed with the idea of bringing a vintage automobile onto the stage. They would drive, stop in a rainstorm, laugh, and find themselves on the deserted and destroyed set of the boulevard. Scenographically, this was quite mad of course, but we knew that the scene needed a driving internal structure, some kind of vehicle that would push it forward. Never afraid of the literal as an opening into the surreal, we discussed dirigibles, hot-air balloons and of course trains. Eventually we settled on a railway coach—or, more accurately, a soundstage cutaway of a railway coach with a back projection of the passing countryside. Thematically, the scene would explore the strange business and personal costs of making films.

In early August, I got a postcard from Dominique telling me of the death of Arletty: "I was close to talking to Arletty. God took her away. She is in Paradise with Le Vigan, Céline, Brasseur and all the others. Carné has accepted to talk to me on the phone. Maybe I'll see him in person later. I understand that he is very disturbed by her departure." Dominique spoke briefly with Carné; he was not particularly interested in our project, in hearing about it or in helping in any way.

Dominique Serrand (as Marcel Carné) confronts a portrait of Vichy Marshal Pétain. Photograph by Michal Daniel.

Dominique has brought back a hoard of new materials that appeared in the French press after Arletty's death. These materials, and others about Vichy and the occupation, will provide the shape and much of the substance for the Trials of the Purification (Scene 16). Dominique has also brought back an article about the fascist Pierre Drieu La Rochelle, which we will combine with some things from Céline and others for Le Vigan's defense during the trials.

In late August, I finally send a long draft of the Design Meeting (Scene 4) to Steve. The draft follows the plan mapped out in the scenario and incorporates a scene between Carné and Paulvé that Felicity had written earlier in the summer. I know it is too long, but I also know that the others will select what is strongest in it and reshape it as necessary. Steve is working on the Reverie (Scene 8), and Felicity is working on interspersing stories from the 1940s with pieces taken from the film for the Dressing Room and Arrest scenes (Scenes 7 and 9). Steve and I talk by telephone and he faxes me drafts of the various scenes as they are written. The task of compiling the final script has fallen into Steve's lap. He says they are "flip-flopping from scene to scene in a desperate effort to get it all down." Dallas seems impossibly far away from Minneapolis. For the first time I feel cut off from the project when it needs me most. A reading of the script, or as much as we have of it, is scheduled for the first week of September.

September 1992

Amidst the debris and dust of demolition and the heavy construction equipment, the members of Theatre de la Jeune Lune and the principal actors hired for *Children of Paradise* meet under the gas-powered construction lamps in the lobby of the new building for a first reading of Act I of the show. Construction on the building is proceeding on schedule and the company traces the progress towards a new future by the slow advance of the floor across the main space. For this first reading there is maybe ten feet of the floor in place; on subsequent evenings the floor will have advanced by ten or fifteen feet until finally the heavy equipment is removed and the building is turned over fully to our project. "It was inspiring," Eric Jensen recalls, "to watch the show start to come together in equal pace with work on the building. As the construction began to wind down, our show began to take shape." Eric also remembers the script of Act I as "an enormous stack of papers." He recalls Dominique and Steve presenting the script scene by scene: "'It's kind of unclear here,' they'd say, 'but there will be a whole thing here and this will turn into that,' and the rest of us were nodding and taking it on faith that somehow what they were talking and gesturing about made sense to somebody, or someday would."

By mid-September, a draft of the whole of Act II is finally in place and another reading is scheduled. In the intervening weeks the company and principal actors have been working daily through sections of Act I and improvising scenes from Act II as they've come together. Now everyone involved in the project—about thirty or so people in all—is together in the same room for a reading of the full script. The excitement is exhilarating. "The theatre was still in shambles," Steve recalls. "There was still no floor in the main space and the Bobcat was in one corner and everything was covered in six inches of dust and we had to string up lights so we could see to read. And this huge thunderstorm moved in and there was this unbelievable downpour the whole time we were reading. It took forever: four or five hours. By the time we finished reading, the thunderstorm had let up and I rode my bike home. But it started raining again and a car came by and hit a puddle and soaked me like surf at the beach. It was a very cleansing moment, very cathartic, as if at last we were underway." We would continue to trim and restructure the text through to opening night, but at least it was written to a kind of conclusion and its final shape was clear.

The scope, density and sheer bulk of the project continues to trouble us. As rehearsals progress, Steve sits with the script and tries to identify openings, repetitions or moments that might be cut or reworked. The scene in Provence (Scene 3) is completely restructured in rehearsal as Dominique and Vincent, in the roles of Carné and Prévert, relentlessly interrupt Barrault's romantic meanderings every time Bob falters or pauses to breathe. The fourteen years that Bob, Dominique and Vincent have worked together, and the affable energy they bring to this scene of three friends and artists talking casually about art, life and love, supplies the sense of ease, immediacy and conversational irreverence missing in the script. Much of what had been written is unnecessary or irrelevant. The same is true in reverse of the first train station scene between Rosay and Carné. Expositional material is moved from later scenes to this scene to take advantage of the magical energy and power that comes from having Dominique and Barbra alone onstage together.

Dominique is rehearsing the Red Breast and Dressing Room scenes (Scenes 5 and 7) as a series of camera moves that take full advantage of the moving set pieces that he and Vincent have designed. As the scenes are blocked out roughly in the space, actors scamper or clamber or teeter along the beams that indicate where the still unfinished floor will eventually be. Precision is of the essence and Joel Sass has been assigned the mammoth task of tracking the camera moves and set choreography. Unfortunately, the set pieces are still being built, so the cast is pushing around various platforms and boxes that bear little resemblance to the scenic pieces they represent. Marketing Director Steve Richardson recalls that every time he came down to watch rehearsal, they seemed to be rehearsing the end of the Provence and Red Breast scenes (Scenes 3–5). He remembers thinking: "This is amazing. I wonder who will come and see it."

Meanwhile, Dominique's cousin, Charlotte Serrand, has arrived from Paris to assist Vincent in the construction and decoration of the models, set pieces and drops for the show. As each piece nears completion it is immediately incorporated into rehearsals to give the actors a clearer sense of what they will be working with and what the various scenes will look like. Similarly, Trina's costumes are being incorporated into rehearsals as they are finished and Chan has been bringing in various musical themes for Eric to begin experimenting with. "By the time we got into rehearsals," Steve Epp recalls, "the whole thing was so complex and dense that even the smallest change or cut meant reconfiguring everything—set movements, costumes changes, everything. There were always three thousand things that every change impacted, making it impossible or at least very difficult to bring the text into line with our three-hour goal."

October 1992

I arrange to attend rehearsals the first weekend of October, and they plan to run through the play, or large blocks of it, to try to get some sense of where we are. It takes all of Saturday to get through Act I; we work through parts of Act II on Sunday. Some sections of the play have never been rehearsed and are only preliminarily blocked. A new and much revised version of the Design Meeting (Scene 4), for example, is introduced for the first time. Other sections—notably the Red Breast (Scene 5) and Dressing Room (Scene 7)—have begun to find a dynamic shape. Sarah Corzatt tells me about the first time she rehearsed the part in Scene 7 in which the young actress Maria Casarès breaks down on camera because she's so nervous she can't keep her hands from shaking: "I really couldn't remember my lines," Sarah admits, "and everyone was staring at me and laughing. It was horrible. I started to cry and it made me mad because Joel [as Director of Photography] was making fun of me because I couldn't remember my lines. He was so mean." Joel later improvised the line about getting a glare "off that chin of hers" and the scene was complete. Unfortunately, the Air Raid (Scene 12) is still an absolute mess and will have to be completely restructured. At present it is a one-act surrealist play in itself. The Peerless Panorama dolly and Arriflex camera have arrived from Film in the Cities. This exquisite piece of machinery gives new meaning to the scope and shape of the show and makes immediate sense of the intricately choreographed blocking of the set pieces that Dominique has arranged with such minute precision.

People seem to be holding up surprisingly well, given all of the energy demanded by this show, the pace at which everyone is working, and the number of distractions associated with opening the new building. We return home after rehearsal in the early hours of the morning and Dominique retreats to the contemplative autumn silence of his garden, where he sits alone in thought for several hours. Over the next several weeks, the parts begin to come together into a whole. Joel continues to track the camera moves from his perch on the camera dolly, and Dominique has begun directing from onstage, fitting himself into the movements of camera and crew as the director of the film, as well as director of the play. David Herskovits has arrived to observe rehearsals as part of his year as a recipient of a Theatre Communications Group Young Directors Fellowship. He immediately volunteers to assist as an outside eye at rehearsals to allow Dominique to spend more time onstage. The assistance he provides in coordinating crew and camera movements and helping to solve logistical problems along the way proves as valuable as his good humor and artistic support.

Joel is designing the costumes and choreographing the chorus for the opening scene on the boulevard. Originally, we had discussed chickens and rabbits in the lobby and maybe some boulevard vendors. The new focus is on underscoring the violence and potential disorder on the street of many murders. The parade of the street enters the lobby as a disruptive chorus of quasi-modern street

Cast and crew evacuate the set when the Allies invade Sicily. Sarah Corzatt (as Maria Casarès) and Charles Schuminski (as Marcel Herrand). Photograph by Michal Daniel.

people, prostitutes, pimps, con men and drug addicts, led by the "angel" (Laura Esping, who also plays Mimi) on eight-foot stilts. The Boulevard scene is trimmed down again as we begin to realize that establishing the atmosphere is more important than textual exposition. Because this scene involves all the extras, it can only be rehearsed at night or on weekends.

On Halloween, Jeune Lune gives a party to inaugurate their new space. Admission is limited by the fire marshal to about a thousand. Everyone is talking about *Children of Paradise*, which will preview November 6 and 7, and open on November 18. We've just gotten word that *Time* magazine reviewer William A. Henry III will attend the opening.

November 1992

The run-through on the Sunday after Halloween takes the whole day. Still, this is a significant improvement over the last weekend rehearsal I attended. The play is long and complicated, but everything is there and there are moments of incredible beauty. After rehearsal, Steve, Dominique and I retreat to a nearby café and talk through everything: music, lights, scenography, character moments, set movements. We settle on a half-dozen places where fairly significant cuts can be made that will only minimally alter what is already in place. These include cutting about six more minutes from the Boulevard scene and another six minutes or so from the Design Meeting (including the intrusion of the Vichy militia that send Trauner and Kosma into the cellar). In some cases cuts are made because the actors hired for minor roles and as extras can't make the moments work; in other cases, little gems are cut because they have become excessive or repetitive.

For me, the major revelation of the weekend is the sudden prominence given to François Truffaut (who had been introduced earlier in the rehearsal process as the source of a simple joke). Now Truffaut, who has been present throughout as a member of the crew, speaks an epilogue to our piece in which he admits with the enthusiasm of youth that he was only a child when *Les Enfants du Paradis* was shot and so was not involved in its making at all. The Truffaut epilogue raises the whole issue of presence and absence in the construction of history and turns our project in the closing minutes on its head, reminding our audience that in all forms of representation nothing is as its seems. Truffaut was of the younger generation of French filmmakers who had rejected Carné only to acknowledge late in his life that he would have traded all his films "to be able to sign my name to *Les Enfants du Paradis*." In our epilogue, he speaks of passing the baton of culture on to the next generation so that "when the next time of darkness comes, those who come after us will do as we have done, and rather than lose what they have, learn it." The simplicity and elegance of this moment is a revelation for me, reconfirming the extent to which we have held to some of the earliest decisions about this project.

We knew from early on that we wanted to end our show with an epilogue that moved beyond our story to speak earnestly and directly about recognizing our debts and continuing on with the struggle to create art that is meaningful and timely. The debt that Truffaut and his generation owed to Carné is similar to the debt that all of us, and especially Dominique, owe to Truffaut. "Besides, there was something beautiful," Steve recalls, "about having the closing statement in our play spoken by Ben [Kernan], the youngest member of the cast." The epilogue itself was compiled from passages in Truffaut's biography and from the film *Fahrenheit 451*. "Mostly," Steve recalls, "I just made it up." It's that simple confession, finally, that confirms the artistry of our work.

November 18, 1992

I arrive at the Minneapolis/St. Paul airport at 7:35 p.m. on opening night and grab a cab toward downtown for the 8:00 curtain. If there is no traffic and the weather is good, the trip from the airport takes twenty-two minutes. Tonight there is a light drizzle that will turn to snow by the time the show is over. We make good time. I enter the lobby with my suitcase just as the opening drum of the prologue sounds. I sit three and a half hours in paradise. I have never been so thrilled by anything I have worked on. It is magic.

Even on opening night, there are surprises. The show has tightened up considerably since I saw it last. I was told the second preview had lasted just over four hours. More cuts have been made, and other changes too. I am shocked by the strong effect on both me and the audience of the projected captions that close the show by tracing the journey of each of our central characters beyond the 1940s. The result is extraordinary. In addition, beautifully articulate speeches have been added to the Trial scene for Carné and Rosay to sum up these characters and pinpoint the thematic importance we have given throughout to letting artists speak out. As Carné talks of "the atrocious feeling of loneliness" that surrounded the making of this film, I think of Dominique sitting late into the night in his garden. The Reverie scene has been completely restructured: the train coach and film projection have been replaced by an exquisite moment in which Carné manipulates and adjusts two film lamps to capture Madame Rosay in the light reflected from the dressing-room mirror, filtered through a bouquet of flowers left over from the previous scene. The magic we have worked so hard to capture is ultimately very simple.

The initial response from the Minneapolis critics is cautiously laudatory. "Jeune Lune's brave effort needs focus" is the headline for Mike Steele's review in the *Minneapolis Star Tribune*: "There's a powerful play somewhere inside this *Children of Paradise* that doesn't emerge, diffused as it is by sheer quantity. Yet watching this troupe wrestle with it is a powerful experience—purely theatrical power—in a space that resonates with creative dynamism" (November 20, 1992). *St. Paul Pioneer Press* reviewer Erin Hart concurs: "*Children of Paradise* is a rambling, impressionistic work that is at times arresting, but never absorbing. Yet it is obviously a labor of love, not just for the art and the people it depicts, but for its audience, as well" (November 21, 1992). The reviewers seem more impressed by the new building than by its inaugural play. The next day, a message in the form of a quotation from Prévert appears on the green-room bulletin board: "I'm tired of slaving for ten months on a screenplay only to be abused in ten lines by some cretin of a critic!"

We know our play is enormous and enormously demanding. But we are confident that we have succeeded in honoring the challenge we set for ourselves in the lines spoken by Jacques Prévert in the Design Meeting: "We must trust our audience most of all. . . . This collaboration, the collaboration of art, is the greatest act of love there is. A banquet of trust. An orgy of respect." Those lines are themselves a poetic paraphrase of the opening lines of Jeune Lune's credo: "We are a theatre of directness, a theatre that speaks to the audience, that listens and needs its response." And the response of the opening-night audience to *Children of Paradise: Shooting a Dream* is both gratifying and inspiring.

Felicity Jones and Robert Rosen. Photograph by Michal Daniel.

Paul Walsh is a freelance dramaturg, adapter and translator. He has worked with Theatre de la Jeune Lune in Minneapolis since 1988 on projects such as Children of Paradise, Germinal, Don Juan Giovanni *and* The Hunchback of Notre Dame. *He taught theatre history and critical studies at Southern Methodist University in Dallas, TX, and is now the Literary Manager at the American Conservatory Theater in San Francisco, CA.*

SELECT BIBLIOGRAPHY

Ariotti, Philippe, and Philippe de Comes. *Arletty*. Paris: Henri Veyrier, 1978.

Armes, Roy. *French Cinema*. London: Secker and Wargurg, 1985.

Asema, Jean-Pierre. *From Munich to the Liberation, 1938–1944*. Translated by Janet Lloyd. Cambridge: Cambridge University Press, 1984.

Baignères, Claude. "Arletty: 'J'suis pas banale!'," *Le Figaro*, 25–26 July 1992, p. 32.

Baldrick, Robert. *The Life and Times of Frederick Lemaître*. London: Hamilton, 1959.

Barrault, Jean-Louis. *Réflexions sur le théâtre*. Paris: Vautrain, 1949.

———. *Memories for Tomorrow*. Translated by Jonathan Griffin. New York: Dutton, 1974.

Barsacq, Leon. *Le décor de film 1895–1969*. Paris: Henri Veyrier, 1985.

———. *Caligari's Cabinet and Other Grand Illusions: A History of Film Design*. Revised and edited by Elliott Stein. Boston: New York Graphic Society, 1976.

Bazin, André. *French Cinema of the Occupation and Resistance*. Translated by Stanley Hochma. New York: Frederick Unger, 1981.

Beaulieu, Henri. *Les théâtres du Boulevard du Crime*. Paris: H. Daragon, 1905.

Berthomé, Jean-Pierre. *Alexander Trauner: Décors de cinéma*. Paris: Jade-Flammarion, 1988.

Bertin-Maghit, Jean-Pierre. *Le cinéma sous l'occupation*. Paris: Olivier Orban, 1989.

Brasseur, Pierre. *Ma vie en vrac*. Paris: Calmann-Levy, 1972.

Brécourt-Villars, Claudine. *Le mots d'Arletty*. Paris: V & O Editions, n.d.

Brown, Frederick. *Theater and Revolution: The Culture of the French Stage*. New York: Viking, 1980.

Cain, Georges. *Anciens théâtres de Paris: Le Boulevard du Temple*. Paris: n.p., 1906.

Champfleury. *Souvenirs des Funambules*. Paris: M. Levy, 1859.

Camus, Albert. *Notebooks, 1942–1951*. Translated by Justin O'Brien. New York: Paragon, 1991.

——. *The Plague*. Translated by Stuart Gilbert. New York: Knopf, 1948.

Carné, Marcel. *Les enfants du paradis: A Film*. Classic Film Scripts. Translated by Dinah Brooke. London: Lorrimer, 1968.

——. *La vie à belles dents: Souvenirs*. Paris: Editions Belfond, 1989.

——. *Les visiteurs du soir*. Bibliotheque des Classiques du Cinema. Paris: Ballard, 1974.

Carné, Marcel, and Jacques Prévert. *Le jour se lève*. Classic Film Scripts. Translated by Dinah Brooke and Nicola Hayden. London: Lorrimer, 1970.

Casarès, Maria. *Residente privilegiée*. Paris: Fayard, 1980.

Colmant, Marie. "Sans Arletty," *Libération*, 25–26 July 1992, p. 27–34.

Desnos, Robert. *Fortunes*. Paris: Gallimard, 1945.

Duras, Marguerite. *The War: A Memoir*. Translated by Barbara Bray. New York: Pantheon, 1986.

Ehrlich, Evelyn. *Cinema of Paradox: French Filmmaking Under the German Occupation*. New York: Columbia University Press, 1985.

"Enquête sur le retour d'une idéologie," *L'Express*, 9 July 1992.

Feyder, Jacques, and Françoise Rosay. *Le cinéma, notre métier*. Vesenaz-pres-Genève: P. Cailler, 1944.

Gascar, Pierre. *Le Boulevard du Crime*. Paris: Hachette, 1986.

Gasiglia-Laster, Danièle. *Jacques Prévert*. Paris: Garamont-Birr, 1986.

Gautier, Theophile. "A Study of Hands." In *The Works of Theophile Gautier*, vol. 24. New York: Spioul, 1903.

Gilson, René. *Jacques Prévert: Des mots et merveilles*. Paris: Belfond, 1990.

Guitry, Sacha. *Deburau*. English version by Harley Granville Barker. New York: Putnam, 1921.

Janin, Jules. *Deburau*. Translated by Winifred Katzin. New York: McBride, 1928.

"Jeune gens, c'était ça la France de Vichy," *L'Evenement du Jeudi*, 23–29 April 1992.

Knapp, Bettina. *Céline: Man of Hate*. Birmingham: University of Alabama Press, 1974.

———. *Louis Jouvet, Man of the Theatre.* New York: Columbia University Press, 1957.

Kozik, Frantisek. *The Great Debureau.* Translated by Dora Reed. New York: Farrar and Rinehart, 1940.

Lacenaire, Pierre-François. *Mémoires de Lacenaire.* New edition. Paris: A. Michel, 1968.

Péricaud, Louis. *Le Théâtre des Funambules.* Paris: L. Sapin, 1897.

Prévert, Jacques. *Choses et autres.* Paris: Gallimand, 1972.

———. *Jenny; Le quai des brumes: scenarios.* Paris: Gallimand, 1988.

———. *Paroles.* Paris: Gallimand, 1957.

———. *Words for All Seasons.* Translated by Teo Savory. Greensboro, NC: Unicorn, 1979.

Prévert, Jacques, and André Pozner. *Hebdromadaires.* Paris: Gallimard, 1982.

Queval, Jean. *Jacques Prévert.* Paris: Mercure de France, 1955.

Rosay, Françoise. *La traversée d'une vie.* Paris: R. Laffont, 1974.

Rousso, Henry. *The Vichy Syndrome.* Translated by Arthur Goldhammer. Cambridge, MA: Harvard University Press, 1991.

Sartre, Jean-Paul. *Being and Nothingness.* Translated by Hazel E. Barnes. New York: Washington Square Press, 1969.

———. *Existentialism.* Translated by Bernard Frechtman. New York: Philosophical Library, 1947.

———. *Nausea.* Translated by Lloyd Alexander. Norfolk, CT: New Directions, 1969.

———. *The War Diaries of Jean-Paul Sartre: November 1939–March 1940.* Translated by Quintin Hoare. New York: Pantheon, 1984.

Seller, Geneviere. *Les enfants du paradis: Etude critique.* Paris: Nathan, 1992.

Seruat, Henry-Jean. "Notre grande Arletty," *Paris Match*, 6 August 1992, p. 38–59.

Siclier, Jacques. *La France de Pétain et son cinéma.* Paris: Henri Veyrier, 1981.

Truffaut, François. *Correspondence 1945–1984.* Edited by Gilles Jacob and Claude de Givray. Translated by Gilbert Adair. New York: Noonday, 1989.

Turk, Edward Baron. *Child of Paradise: Marcel Carné and the Golden Age of French Cinema.* Cambridge, MA: Harvard University Press, 1989.

———. "The Birth of *Children of Paradise*," *American Film*, July–August 1979, p. 43–49.